FAITH...

STANDING...

Written by Luanne Scrogan

Jeremiah 17:8
For he shall be as a tree planted by the waters, and that spreadeth out her roots by the river, and shall not see when heat cometh, but her leaf shall be green; and shall not be careful in the year of drought, neither shall cease from yielding fruit.

A journey to non-wavering trust and faith in God, despite the odds that say there is no hope!

ISBN-13: 978-1-7324804-0-7

Job 14:7
For there is hope of a tree, if it be cut down, that it will sprout again, and that the tender branch thereof will not cease.

God Bless,
Asking in Faith
... Nothing Wavering! James 1:6

4

All stories and facts in this book are true; scriptures and other quotes are offered for edification, clarification and study purposes.
Unless otherwise indicated, Bible quotations are referenced from the King James version (KJV) for ease of word study purposes in alignment with original Greek and Hebrew definitions. Quotations from other bible translations are as marked.

Printed by Trinity Press, Norcross Georgia
First printing June 2018
Paperback

At the current time additional books can be ordered by contacting us at: faithstanding@protonmail.com

Photography by: **Samantha Alice Groves**

ISBN-13: 978-1-7324804-0-7

Author's Notes:
By: Luanne Scrogan

"Faith Standing"
Where It all began:
It was all too many years ago that God first impressed upon my heart the importance of writing down my testimonies of His faithfulness. When He began prodding me about it, He was relentless! I procrastinated though, far too long; but when I finally surrendered to His call and began to "jot down" testimonies of His faithfulness (as I would recall them), my own faith was increasingly encouraged! Most of the testimonies shared here are personal ones; however, there are some shared testimonies of family and friends.

As I wrote I could sense the peaceful presence of the Holy Spirit, it was an amazing journey! Early on, He began to guide me into something much deeper as He impressed on me the importance of scriptural support for the reader's better understanding. I began to see that He did not plan for me to write this just for my own edification, but also that others could read it and be encouraged to stand in faith. With clearer understanding of God's word on this subject, others can learn and find the confidence and spiritual strength to trust God!

Only carefully with the Holy Spirit's guidance was this book written. I pray that each person that has chosen to study this with me will come to realize that we do not have to be "pillars" in the eyes of man in order to be a "pillar" of faith before God. In other words, man will quite often strive to alter situations in order to satisfy his own will and desires. Therefore, you must not measure your own ability and faith by man's limited opinion of you. God and His word must be our measuring stick. However, we must also remember that, although *man can most certainly persuade the powerful hand of God to move; God is **not** subject to man's approval or even man's attempts at manipulation. God works according to **His** will.*

"He who overcomes, I will make him a pillar in the temple of My God, and he shall go out no more. And I will write on him the name of My God and the name of the city of My God...

What is faith?

I have come to realize that:

*Faith dances with great joy at planting, ...
in great expectation of the harvest's increase!*

**Please continue on with me
and by the time we're done,
this will be your song of faith!**

Warning: This book contains many tools of faith! Putting them to use will increase one's determination and spiritual strength and tenacity to STAND IN FAITH and TRUST GOD! One may also find themselves standing on faith completely and unwaveringly, which could become habit forming and spread to others. It can lead to daily praise and worship of the Almighty and should be monitored regularly for miraculous wonders and victorious joy! It is advised that a journal be kept so that one's progress might be monitored and treated more efficiently and referenced by the Great Physician as needed.
Possible side effects: One might also become a public testimony of God's faithfulness!

Special Thanks to:

Ken Scrogan – My loving husband for your loving support and patience. I will never forget the excitement and interest that you showed after reading the first 9 pages! It gave me the encouragement that I need to continue on!

Florence McHaffie – For encouraging me to take that first step that led me into this journey of Faith Standing!

Terry deLeon – My wonderful supporting sister! You have always been there for me and I couldn't ask for a better sister! Thank you so much for spending the time to edit, proof read and critique this work, you did an amazing job! Most of all for your encouragement which picked me up and gave me the confidence to keep going when I felt like surrendering!

Laura Sides – My wonderful God loving mom! Although she is no longer here with us, her help editing the first few chapters helped me in so many ways! Her wisdom and positive critique helped me throughout my writing. I love you and miss you mom!

Photography: Samantha Alice Groves – Great job! Thank you!

Dorothy Mathews – Thank you for our long visits and discussions about this work over coffee in the early days. Your ability to relate bible story applications were priceless and so helpful!

Pastors Chuck Slater and Cameron King – For encouraging and allowing me to step out and be myself! For helping me grow in confidence, and how to rise above fear of mistakes or feelings of inadequacy!

Contents

How to Begin

During the writing of this book, I found myself in the middle of many situations that tested my faith beyond my own endurance. But the assurance that God truly loves me unconditionally and that He is faithful to the very end, kept me within His grasp. He has always been there, speaking to my spirit, offering to me His guidance and wisdom and His promise to bring me through whatever difficulties I face. I wish I could say that I have always listened well to Him and been as faithful to Him as He is to me, but alas; I fall short time and again, letting the cares of this life pull me into turmoil and all manner of struggles. I found that until you finally decide to truly turn to Him and surrender yourself; that you will remain in the midst of the battle! It is then that you can find Him ready to forgive and lift you up. He truly is my source of strength and joy. Without Him I would easily be reduced to a tub of goo!

Throughout the writing and study of Faith Standing, the Holy Spirit continued to give me sweet guidance. I personally began to grow in my own faith; and as my understanding grew, my relationship with the Lord became increasingly exciting! Jesus grew in my heart and I felt stronger in my faith walk than ever before.

Personally, when it comes to studying things that I really want to grasp hold of, I am a "digger". When I study the word of God, I can't help myself; I must dig deeper and deeper until I come to a clear and precise understanding of what I am reading or hearing. So, as you enter this faith-building offering, you will notice that I have included various word translations for you. I offer these translations for your convenience and hope that you will put them to good use for your own complete understanding and encouragement. I also hope that they will encourage you to also become a "digger", to help you learn and grow in all the good things that God places in your heart to do.

Have you ever experienced a time when you read a scripture passage that taught you a wonderful lesson and then upon rereading the same passage again later, you found that the same passage offered another completely different lesson? God is so good; His word is written so that we can learn so much more than what is just on the surface.

10

God's word never changes but fits so many applications within the same scripture! It is truly miraculous! Makes me think of a kaleidoscope; same set of crystals, but they appear differently, depending on where they are pointed.

Quite often, full understanding is limited by a lack of clear and precise defining of a word. You might say it gets "Lost in the translation". The word of God is so incredible! Understanding is typically characterized and applied according to the need of the individual seeking for meaning at the given time. Some might find the translations offered in this book a bit overwhelming; I recommend using them as you have need, digging only as deep as you need to, for your clear and complete understanding. As a digger, as-in so many aspects of life; I find that over digging can lead onto rabbit trails that might cause the student to lose the point altogether, I must stay focused! Not all individuals relate to things in the same way. For example: Some portions of a word's meaning might bring one to a deeper understanding of God's character; whereas another reader will apply the same meaning to something more personal. The word of God should never be limited by only one person's application, it's a personal thing and heavenly inspired. So, when applied to one's personal life, God's word will always lead into a deeper understanding of God Himself, as well as a deeper personal relationship with Him. Remember, we are not discussing doctrines here, we are talking personal *spiritual inspiration and application.* God, the Holy Spirit, is the teacher; we are His students and subjects.

Digging: This in-depth study of God's word, helps us to understand that, when words are translated from one language to another, there can sometimes be more than one meaning for that word with totally different applications. For example, the word "meek", when translated from the King James English, can refer to a very humble person (i.e. Jesus), or it can be referring to a poor, lowly, pathetic individual (i.e. a homeless person, drug addict, or a sickly person, etc.). In either case the meaning that would be applied is determined by the subject at hand and how it is used in its context. This is why word searches are so very important. PLEASE NOTE: Contrary to what many in the world have said; it is not the Bible that is flawed; it is our understanding that is all too often flawed and in error. When

11

we understand the translated word's true meaning, our understanding is revealed!

Therefore, the study guides in Faith Standing are primarily complete translations of scripture; derived from The Strong's Exhaustive Concordance. It was done this way in order to offer to you (the reader), full opportunity to study the word of God from a "digger's" perspective! Study as deep as you choose, either way, you will grow in your understanding and also in your faith!

The King James translation is primarily the bible source I have used for the scriptures found in Faith Standing, unless otherwise noted. The translations offered in this book can be found in Strong's Concordance/Dictionary which works in conjunction with the King James Translation.

Side note for clarification: Years ago, we had an exchange student from Japan staying with us. When we introduced "Wataru"; to American tacos for the first time, he began to snicker a little. I asked, what is so funny? He then explained: "Japan also has the word 'taco', but it has a different meaning. It has two meanings! The word 'taco' in Japanese can mean 'kite' (like the kind you fly in the sky), or it can mean 'octopus'." Yes, you got it right! It could mean either word, dependent on the application at the time. So, you can see how the understanding can be so easily lost or totally misunderstood in the translating from one language to another. King James English and American English can differ quite a lot at times. Sometimes, we have to understand some things about the translator and their own culture before it becomes clear.

One important note: The translations noted in Faith Standing were carefully chosen. They are only for those words that I felt, were in need of deeper study for clearer understanding of their meaning and the specific application at hand. You will relate more to this as you move along into the study. If you find the translations overwhelming or distracting to the flow of the discussion and subject at hand, I might suggest you mark the area and dig deeper at a later time. However, I would suggest you always take at least a quick look at the words and translations offered so you can follow along with clearer understanding! Remember to make notes at those points you wish to review and perhaps study deeper at a later time.

Pray always, for guidance and wisdom each day as you begin. As you enter this journey, my desire is that you learn and grow in your faith, so that you can also grow in your relationship with God and have the confidence that you need to stand before the world and state clearly,

"For I know who I believe,
and I am persuaded that He is able
to keep that which I have committed to Him...
...today and every day!"

Plant your seeds along the road and keep watching for the harvest!

In Christ's Love,
Luanne Scrogan

Section 1-

FAITH......
STANDING...

Written by: Luanne Scrogan

What is faith? I've come to realize that:

Faith dances with great joy at planting,
In great expectation...
...of the harvest's increase!

Years ago, we planted our first vegetable garden and as I think back about it, I never even considered the possibility of ending up with nothing in the end! I fully expected to have a generous harvest. It was a very large garden!

We did experience a few normal garden setbacks, but still had an abundance of food! I remember my young grandson, walking through the garden and picking green tomatoes off the vine. He would take a bite and toss it to the ground as the sour-bitter taste hit his palate! I made my way to him as quickly as I could and did my best to guide him in his choices as he continued to forage the garden for a better choice! Cucumbers were in abundance and grew so fast we couldn't keep up! We had such fun taking pictures of our little 3-year-old gardener holding a cucumber that could be easily mistaken for a watermelon in his tiny hands!

As I placed a large colorful bowl of nutritious garden treasures on the counter-top, I lifted that sweet boy to sit next to the bowl. He was so excited about all

14

the colorful veggies! However, I had to keep a close eye, as I did my best to limit his choices for tasting! Although I must confess that several pieces required "trimming" due to some curious small bite marks! It was so rewarding to enjoy the fruits of our labors in so many wonderful ways! As I took pictures of the huge bowls and buckets of vegetables I was reminded of the great fun we had planting the seeds and felt such satisfaction in the results before me!

When planting, if you do not look forward with great expectation for a harvest's increase, then I would need to ask, "Why are you preparing a garden? Did you plant seed?" Surely, when a seed is planted, there are expectations for an upcoming harvest! It is not something you just wish for; but, it is something you fully expect!

Continue on with me and by the time we're done the statement above <u>will</u> be your song of faith as well!

Hebrews 11:1 Now faith is the substance of things hoped for, the evidence of things not seen. {substance: or, ground, or, confidence} (KJV)

What does this really mean?
Well, I am somewhat of a "digger" and when I study God's word, I like to dig deep for clearer understanding. I have offered some gems from my expeditions in the side margin; come and dig a little with me, and let's learn as much as we can from what the Bible teaches about STANDING IN FAITH!

What manner of prayer do you suppose will exercise our Faith? Sometimes we come begging and pleading, crying out in hopeless desperation; "O Please, O Please I beg of you God...! At times, we try to negotiate; "God, if you meet this need, I

Study Notes:

Let's Dig
--Interlinear (with Greek):
"Now <de> faith <pistis> is <esti> the substance <hupostasis> of things hoped for <elpizo>, the evidence <elegchos> of things<pragma> not <ou> seen <blepo>."

Let's Dig: (Hebrews 11:1)
--**Faith <pistis>, pis'-tis** = persuasion, i.e. credence; moral conviction:-- assurance, belief, believe, faith, fidelity.

--**Substance <hupostasis>, hoop-os'-tas-is** = a setting under (support), i.e. (figuratively) concretely, essence, confidence,

--**Hoped for <elpizo>el-pid'-zo** = to expect or confide: trust.

--**Evidence <elegchos> el'-eng-khos** = proof, conviction:--evidence, reproof.

will…!   Or the pie-crust-promise prayer: "I won't…bla-bla…ever again." Begging! Pleading! Whining and dealing! Doesn't sound like faith to me! Sounds more like a whining cry of desperation and hopelessness! Perhaps it could be described best as: "a lonely cry of *doubt* at the moment of desperation!" Let's be honest, we have all experienced those kinds of moments! However, the word of God indicates that pure Faith carries more confidence than that! In fact, I discovered that Faith is a stable and unwavering trust! Frankly it is just <u>not willing to entertain</u> doubts and feelings of desperation!

When we ask God, in Faith-<u>believing,</u> we recognize where the answer to prayer comes from. But we enter that prayer of faith, <u>knowing</u> that we are putting our petition before an almighty faithful God, while trusting in **His** great mercy and love. We stand in confidence, in **Him**, that it **is** taken care of. **Faith** therefore, is thankful and grateful; not willing to give up! In taking this stand, our hope gains a great foundation because of its master builder. The tears that flow now, are tears of hope, adoration, thankfulness, love, humility, and all of those things that flow from a grateful trusting heart.

"But I still shed tears when I pray?" Tears are basically the body's way of releasing tension and are very cleansing. They are not necessarily an indication of doubt and in fact, can more often be an indication of a release of self! I'm reminded of the tears that are provoked by the comfort of a caring friend at the moment of someone's sorrow. The emotional burst of relief to know that you don't have to bear your burden alone; can lighten the load immensely! Think back, can you remember a time like that?

16

Have you ever sat and watched a squirrel running up and down the trees and jumping from branch to branch? They barely stop to consider how strong or how far the next branch is; they just jump and leap and grab! If they begin to fall they just reach out and grab; they are confident in who they are and in the abilities that they have been given! Truly amazing!

> *Romans 8:24-25*
> *For we are saved by hope: but hope that is seen is not hope: for what a man seeth, why doth he yet hope for?*
> *v.25) But if we hope for that we see not, then do we with patience wait for it.*

We see here that Faith (in God) is a <u>cheerful</u> trust, with *anticipation* of the answers to those petitions that we have set before Him. But don't forget to include the required dosage of endurance and an <u>unwavering refusal to give up</u>! I think that's pretty exciting!

Things may look hopeless, but; **"...we walk by <u>faith</u>, not by sight"**. (See **2 Corinthians 5:7**)

NOT ALLOWING CIRCUMSTANCES TO DICTATE OUR LEVEL OF FAITH.

...Taking on a Positive Mental Attitude, keeping your thoughts on God and His faithfulness and not on the circumstances.

> *Isaiah 26:3*
> *Thou wilt keep him in perfect peace, whose mind is stayed on thee: because he trusteth in thee.*

I get so excited when I can gain more clear understanding of the word of God through searching

---

Study Notes:

Let's Dig: (Romans 8:24-25)

--Hope <elpis> el-pece' = to anticipate, usually with pleasure; expectation or confidence, faith.

--Patience <hupomone> hoop-om-on-ay' = cheerful (or hopeful) endurance, constancy:--enduring, patience, patient continuance (waiting).
From the word:
--hupomeno, hoop-om-en'-o = to stay under (behind), i.e. remain; to undergo, i.e. bear (trials), have fortitude, persevere, i.e. remain.

Let's Dig: (Isaiah 26:3)
(Ponder slowly, if you will, on the root meanings of these Hebrew words)
- Keep -natsar, naw-tsar' = a primitive root; to guard, in a good sense (to protect, maintain)
- Perfect and Peace are the same word - shalowm, shaw-lome' or shalom = safe, i.e. (figuratively) well, happy, friendly; also (abstractly) welfare, i.e. health, prosperity, peace, favour, + friend.
From the root word:
--shalam, shaw-lam' = a primitive root; to be safe (in mind, body or estate)
-- Mind -yetser, yay'-tser = a form; figuratively, conception (i.e. purpose):-- frame, thing framed, imagination, mind, work.
From the word –
--yatsar, yaw-tsar' = to mould into a form; especially as a potter; figuratively, to determine (i.e. form a resolution), purpose.

out the original meanings of the words! With this added understanding, we can really see what God is trying to teach us through His word. We learned that God will guard and protect us. You can be safe, happy, healthy and prosperous in spirit, mind, soul, and body; if you will only fill your mind with the goodness of God and set your sights on what **He** has set before you. If you will hold on to Him, lean on Him; putting self totally and completely into His care; in the midst of good or bad. Standing also in confidence that **He will** make a way; **He will** meet your need, and **He will** keep what you commit to Him! You do not need to be concerned about the circumstances and cares of this life, but only take each day and each event one step at a time; letting **Him** lead the way... and.... **He will!**

Okay, okay! I didn't say it was going to be as easy as pie! Although making a pie is not always that easy! It's not that easy to put self aside either. But the first step is looking to God, getting to know Him and recognizing that this life, here and now is temporal! We have to recognize also that our spiritual existence is eternal; this is key to letting go of those things in this life that so easily hold us back. So now, what's really important?

2 Corinthians 4:18
While we look not at the things which are seen, but at the things which are not seen: for the things which are seen are temporal; but the things which are not seen are eternal.

Take a moment and re-read this passage. Insert the words *"Consider carefully that"*, in place of the word *"While"*.

"Consider carefully that" *we look not at the things which are seen, but at the things which are not seen:*

Study Notes:

-- Stayed - camak, saw-mak' = a primitive root; to prop (literally or figuratively); reflexively, to lean upon or take hold of (in a favorable or unfavorable sense):--bear up, stablish, (up-)hold, lay, lean, lie hard, put, rest self, set self, stand fast, stay (self), sustain.

-- Trusteth - batach, baw-takh' = a primitive root; properly, to hie for refuge, figuratively, to trust, be confident or sure:--be bold (confident, secure, sure), careless (one), put confidence, (make to) hope, (put, make to) trust.

(2 Cor. 4:18)
-- **While <skopeo> skop-eh'-o** = to take aim at (spy), regard:--consider, take heed, look at (on), mark.
From the word
  --skopos, skop-os' from skeptomai = (to peer about ("skeptic"), a watch (sentry or scout), i.e. (by implication) a goal:--mark

18

for the things which are seen are temporal; but the things which are not seen are eternal.

Hummm, it's kind of interesting to take note of what happens in your brain when you send a message to <u>Consider</u> or <u>give regard to</u> something. Kind of makes you sit-up and pay attention!

> ***Proverbs 16:3*** *Commit thy works unto the LORD, and thy thoughts shall be established.*

As we commit everything that we do to the Lord, he will help us with our thought processes. I found the following quote that says it quite nicely:

> ***"A man who puts aside his trust in Christ because he is going into society is like one taking off his shoes because he is about to walk upon thorns."*** --Unknown

"When the going gets rough, the tough get going"? Right? When do you need God the most? Absolutely when things are rough; but all too often our tendency is to put all our focus on trying to control the situation and we let our faith and our trust in God fall by the wayside. We push our faith and God to the back seat; or even push them completely out the window, while **<u>we</u>** drive on down the road, struggle on our own with the issues and problems that face us! What kind of faith is that!?

For all too many years, I could not understand why I didn't seem to <u>ever</u> have enough faith. It even crossed my mind that perhaps faith is given only in

Study Notes:

Let's Dig: **(Proverbs 16:3)**
Commit - galal, gaw-lal' =
a primitive root; to roll (literally or figuratively):-- commit, remove, roll (away, down, together), run down, seek occasion, trust, wallow.

Works - ma`aseh, mah-as-eh' = an action (good or bad); generally, a transaction; abstractly, activity; by implication, a product (specifically, a poem) or (generally) property:--act, art, + bakemeat, business, deed, do(-ing), labor, thing made, ware of making, occupation, thing offered, operation, possession, X well, ((handy-, needle-, net-))work(ing, -manship), wrought.

Thoughts - machashabah, makh-ash-aw-baw' = or machashebeth {makh-ash-eh'-beth}; from 2803; a contrivance, i.e. (concretely) a texture, machine, or (abstractly) intention, plan (whether bad, a plot; or good, advice):--cunning (work), curious work, device(-sed), imagination, invented, means, purpose, thought.
):--cunning (work), curious work, device(-sed), imagination, invented, means, purpose, thought.

...

19

proportionally gifted doses from God? That line of thought brought me to wonder what I needed to do to earn some faith! I wondered what criteria a person had to meet in order to deserve a portion or even a small "dose", it made me feel hopeless at times! Oh, my goofy and vivid imagination! Of course, after some mental review of what I have learned about God and His nature I began to really understand that the Word of God contains the answers to that dilemma! Understanding Him and building our personal relationship with Him is where we can gather "doses" of faith. The keys are laid out there in His word like many "bouquets of roses"! But, it is up to us how much of these wonderful fragrant flowers we collect and claim as ours! It's a matter of getting to know and learning to trust the one who planted the rose garden in the first place! This is the basis of the development of our faith!

At times when my faith seems low, as I assess my self-examination, I find that I've not spent much time in the "rose garden" among the roses! I've not exercised my faith. In other words, I have not spent the quantity of time in God's word, or in prayer, or even in praise and worship of Him that would offer any real quality of nourishment to my soul and spirit. No wonder, I have only noticed the thorns among the roses! We must linger in the garden if we want to see the beauty of the roses and to smell their wonderfully intoxicating fragrance. Running through the garden aimlessly will only cause the thorns to prick you and cause hurt and pain. Let's stop for a moment, look at the beauty of God's word, the wisdom offered there, the peace and wonder of it all. That is where you find faith in abundance!

Study Notes:

... **Established - kuwn, koon =**
a primitive root; properly, to be erect (i.e. stand perpendicular); hence (causatively) to set up, in a great variety of applications, whether literal (establish, fix, prepare, apply), or figurative (appoint, render sure, proper or prosperous):--certain(-ty), confirm, direct, faithfulness, fashion, fasten, firm, be fitted, be fixed, frame, be meet, ordain, order, perfect, (make) preparation, prepare (self), provide, make provision, (be, make) ready, right, set (aright, fast, forth), be stable, (e-)stablish, stand, tarry, X very deed.

20

John 6:63
"It is the Spirit who gives life; the flesh profits nothing. The words that I speak to you are spirit, and they are life.

Psalm 1:1
*Blessed is the man **who** walks **not** in the counsel of the ungodly, **nor** stands in the path of sinners, **nor** sits in the seat of the scornful; 2) But his delight is in the law of the LORD, And in His law, he meditates day and night. 3) He shall be like a tree Planted by the rivers of water, that brings forth its fruit in its season, whose leaf also shall not wither; And whatever he does shall prosper. (see Joshua 1:8 & 9)*

Remember my song of Faith?

Faith dances with great joy at planting,
In great expectation of the harvest's increase!

Meditate carefully on the following scripture, and take a moment to consider these thoughts:

Faith is like a muscle; if we want to build that muscle we must exercise it! But also, we have to feed it and give it the building blocks that it needs to grow and repair.

Think about it this way: If you sit around day after day and get no exercise your muscles get weak and can atrophy (lose their muscle tone and strength). On the same token, if you go to the gym and work out hard, maybe even lift some weights; but you don't support these efforts consistently, and with things like the amino acids (the building blocks of protein), antioxidants, and good clean water (for healthy hydration) your muscles will not build. In fact, they will become weak and tired, achy and sore!

What are you doing for your spirit? Is it weak and tired, achy and sore?

Galatians 6:8
For he who sows to his flesh will of the flesh reap corruption, but he who sows to the Spirit will of the Spirit reap everlasting life. 9) And let us not grow weary while doing good, for in due season we shall reap if we do not lose heart.

*How can you expect God to speak to you in that gentle and
inward voice which melts the soul, when you are making
so much noise with your rapid reflections?
Be silent, and God will speak again.
--Francois Fenelon*

Section 2 –

The most incredible Opportunity... ever offered!

Ephesians 2:8 For by grace are ye saved through faith; and that not of yourselves: it is the gift of God (KJV)

As a young believer, I struggled with certain defeating thought patterns. Patterns that life's trials and struggles had set into motion in my mind. I had been led into thinking that the reason why I struggled so hard to gain faith was because there was something wrong with me. I saw and heard how God was blessing other people and answering their prayers; but I couldn't seem to muster up enough faith to believe Him for the answers that I looked for. For some time, I actually considered, that maybe He just wanted me to try and handle things on my own to see if I measured up to be fit for heaven! I even struggled with thoughts that maybe I wasn't really meant to find grace in God. Perhaps, I was "predestined" to be lost. **That** thought pattern just about put me 6ft under! That kind of thinking is so majorly defeating!! Somehow, I knew in my heart that this thought process was **all wrong**, but I still couldn't seem to find my way to a successful walk of faith. I had such a low self-esteem that I even began to dance with the idea that if faith really was a *gift*, and if, in fact it was doled out by God as He saw fit; then perhaps, I just wasn't desirable or valuable enough to fit the criteria that qualified a person for this gift. What a dead-end street!!!

Let's Dig: (Ephesians 2:8)

Grace - charis, khar'-ece = graciousness (as gratifying), of manner or act (abstract or concrete; literal, figurative or spiritual; especially the divine influence upon the heart, and its reflection in the life; including gratitude):--acceptable, benefit, favour, gift, grace(- ious), joy, liberality, pleasure, thank(-s, -worthy).

Saved - swzw sozo, sode'-zo = from a primary sos (contraction for obsolete saos, "safe"); to save, i.e. deliver or protect (literally or figuratively):--heal, preserve, save (self), do well, be (make) whole.

Faith - pistis, pis'-tis = persuasion, i.e. credence; moral conviction (of religious truth, or the truthfulness of God or a religious teacher), especially reliance upon Christ for salvation; abstractly, constancy in such profession; by extension, the system of religious (Gospel) truth itself:--assurance, belief, believe, faith, fidelity.

Gift - doron, do'-ron = a present; specially, a sacrifice:--gift, offering.

God - theos, theh'-os = of uncertain affinity; a deity, especially the supreme Divinity; figuratively, a magistrate; by Hebraism, very:--X exceeding, God, god(-ly, -ward).

24

However, now I know, that this line of thinking is incorrect and extremely destructive! In addition, it would even conflict with Hebrew 11:1; as we discussed in the beginning. Grace is the most important gift that God has offered to us. We receive that gift, through faith, thereby; making the <u>choice</u> to seize the most incredible opportunity ever offered to man!

We are all given a "measure", or a portion of faith; and it is through that measure that our hearts are stirred by the presence of God through His Holy Spirit. By this also, it is hoped that we will choose a relationship with God over the things of this world that would threaten to separate us from Him. However, the measure of faith that God gives to each man must be exercised, otherwise just like that unexercised muscle, it can atrophy and lose its strength. Our measure of faith will tend to atrophy as we push God away and ignore or reject Him.

As I began to awaken to the full reality, in-that grace is a gift; it was a true revelation to my whole being that all we need to do is receive it! God also tells us in His word that if we (any Christian-Believer) lack wisdom, He will give <u>liberally</u> to those that ask for it. He offers us an incredible education through His wisdom and urges us to study it faithfully. He knows that, as we study His word (the Bible, of course) we will not only obtain wisdom, but our faith will be increased and our relationship with Him will be strengthened! If we wish to have our faith and our knowledge of His ways increased and strengthened, we must also spend time in prayer (in conversation with Him). How can you expect to fully trust and/or emulate someone that you hardly know?

While pondering on this subject, I found myself thinking of Popeye the Sailor man. (Truly dating myself!) He would fight his battles on His own until he was just about to lose; completely beaten down and mangled. Than at the point of total desperation, he would pull out that trusty can of spinach; suck it up through his pipe and "ta-da-da-dat-da-da"! He would fill up with power and muscles and win the fight!

Of course, faith isn't a can of spiritual spinach to be yanked out for a boost of faith in times of desperation and discouragement. We also know that Popeye isn't going to jump in and save the day with his can of spinach either! But we do know that, although faith is not made of spinach, a consistent intake of the components of faith are building blocks for your spirit; just as a consistent intake of spinach is for your body!

If you lack faith, perhaps you need more time with God, to discover who He is; and who you are to Him. Go back to God's word, study it. Take the time and dig deeper. Search God's word for deeper meaning and understanding. Ask God for the wisdom and the clear understanding of how to walk in faith! Take a stand and decide to trust Him! Make that choice to truly trust God and exercise that measure of faith that you already possess. He won't let you down! I had begun to see that the primary point is not whether faith is a gift, but that faith must be exercised in order for it to grow and become strong. Yes, by all means; choosing to take that stand of faith requires determination because, when you take that stand the enemy will likely attack you with thoughts of doubt and discouragement. Not to mention that we ourselves can be our own attacker sometimes. This determination requires a firm (even stubborn) refusal to give up and even more exactly; a stark resistance

26

to any contrary thought or circumstance that would threaten to break your stand.

Ephesians 4:7
But unto every one of us is given grace according to the measure of the gift of Christ.

Ponder on all this for a moment. How do we begin to measure such an incredible gift as; Jesus Christ's sacrifice on the cross for our sins? It's measureless! This grace… this offer of salvation is miraculous; in fact, (see our dig notes) Grace is "The divine influence upon the heart."

So, can you imagine, as you ponder the cross and the incredible gift of grace that it bestows; that perhaps **your own level of faith** could become a Mountain Moving Force? I think it can! What a truly exciting thought!

James 1:5-6
*If any of you lack wisdom, let him ask of God, that giveth to all men liberally, and upbraideth not; and it shall be given him. 6 But let him ask **in faith**, <u>nothing wavering</u>. For he that wavereth is like a wave of the sea driven with the wind and tossed.*

Many times, I believe we just **think** too much, we **think** ourselves right out of trusting God. We "reason" ourselves out of our faith and trust!

Romans 12:3
*For I say, through the grace given unto me, to every man that is among you, not to think of himself more highly than he ought to think; but to think soberly, according **as God hath dealt to every man the measure of faith***

Study Notes:
Let's Dig:
(Eph. 4:7)
  Wow! We are given…

--Grace - cariv charis, khar'-ece = graciousness (as gratifying), of manner or act (abstract or concrete; literal, figurative or spiritual; especially <u>the divine influence upon the heart</u>, and its reflection in the life; including gratitude):--acceptable, benefit, favour, gift, grace(- ious), joy, liberality, pleasure, thank(-s, -worthy).
From the word
--chairo, khah'-ee-ro =a primary verb; to be "cheer"ful, i.e. calmly happy or well-off

--Measure - metron, met'-ron = an apparently primary word; a measure ("metre"), literally or figuratively; by implication, a limited portion (degree):--measure.

--Gift - dorea, do-reh-ah' = a gratuity:--gift.
From the word
--doron, do'-ron = a present; specially, a sacrifice:--gift, offering

Let's Dig:
(James 1:5-6)

*--**Wavering (wavereth)= diakrino, dee-ak-ree'-no** = to separate thoroughly, i.e. (literally and reflexively) <u>to withdraw from</u>, or (by implication) oppose; figuratively, to discriminate (by implication, decide), or (reflexively) <u>hesitate</u>:--contend, make (to) differ(-ence), discern, doubt, judge, be partial, <u>stagger</u>, waver.*

We all have that measure of faith that God has
granted us since birth! The bible tells us that all we
need is faith the size of a mustard seed and we could
move mountains! He already gave us that! We have
within us the natural knowledge of our Creator and
even that small amount is all we need to virtually
move mountains! Wow, what an incredible thought!
But what holds us back?

> *"Today's mighty oak is just yesterday's nut
> that held its ground."* – Anonymous

It's a choice. What choice will you make tomorrow,
or next week when the floods of life's trials come
and try to beat you down? Will you choose to water
that seed of faith with God's word? Will you choose
to stand against those floods and trust Him? Can you
allow yourself to believe that He will see you
through it to the very end of the fight? Or will you
let that faith building opportunity pass you by? Don't
let that seed dry up and threaten to decompose.
Water and feed it with the word of God, give it some
Son-shine, and take it for a trial spin! The bible uses
the word "Selah", meaning pause and think about it,
and in the same manner I say "Hummmmm...
WOW"! I find this very thought provoking;
remembering that Faith is like a muscle; unless you
work it, it will stiffen and atrophy. But if you
exercise it, it will build and grow! There are great
rewards in that!

1 Corinthians 3:10
*According to the **grace** of God which was
given to me, as a wise master builder I have
laid the foundation, and another builds on it.
But let each one take heed how he builds on
it.*

28

There was a period of time in our marriage where I felt very neglected. His computer interests had seemingly swallowed him whole and I felt very alone. I felt powerless to find a way to draw him out of this cyber world and I got very discouraged and resentful! I began to feel that my marriage was over. I was a young woman and did not want to live virtually alone for the rest of my life!

My resentment, anger and hopelessness continued to grow for many years and in fact one day, sitting with my mother in tears I announced that I did not see how I could continue to live in this marriage! I felt so angry and felt the love in my heart was gone! I felt numb!

My mother, being the wise woman that she was, gave me this very sound advice: "Your mind is so full of all of the negative things about him that you can't see any of the good; but, you need to ask God to help you see your husband through Jesus' eyes and let Him help you through this!

Well, I guess maybe I'm just stubborn and didn't want to let go of my anger and resentment; but, after another year or so I finally, released my heart to God concerning the matter and asked for His help! The circumstances had not changed but I began to realize that I could not change him, I could only change me. So, I turned my heart to God and asked Him to help me love my husband and see him through The Lord's eyes! It took a little while, because I had to be willing to not dwell on the negative and anger and I had to truly surrender my heart! I began to realize then that God had given me a renewed love for Ken and even more... a determination to give the whole situation to Jesus!

Study Notes:

Was it easy? Not at all! Because I was in a fight with myself and my pride as much as with my husband and his cyber world! But, as I determined in my heart to let The Lord deal with my husband, my own heart began to heal and my relationship with Jesus grew and our marriage gradually improved!

God gave me a renewed heart of grace and unconditional love toward Ken and also helped me to realize that as I turn my problems over to Him, He IS Faithful and JUST to help me through it! Things may not come together as they do in the fairy tales and movies but with God anything is possible! The most important thing to remember from this, I believe is this: When facing Giants, it's not the heart of the giant that has to be changed but the heart of the person that faces it!

David did not beat Goliath because of any change in Goliath's heart; he brought that giant down because he trusted in God to guide him and protect him, and God was faithful! You plant your seed of faith and God will have your back!

Let's take a minute and look at…

The Parable of the Sower.

This chapter in Mark, addresses this issue quite clearly. I chose to insert the whole chapter, because it addresses this subject so well! Please read it carefully and give ear to what Jesus was telling them.

> *Mark 4 (NIV)*
> *Again, Jesus began to teach by the lake. The crowd that gathered around him was so large that he got into a boat and sat in it out on the lake, while all the people were along the shore at the water's edge. 2 He taught*

*them many things by parables, and in his
teaching said: 3 "Listen! A farmer went out
to sow his seed. 4 As he was scattering the
seed, some fell along the path, and the birds
came and ate it up. 5 Some fell on rocky
places, where it did not have much soil. It
sprang up quickly, because the soil was
shallow. 6 But when the sun came up, the
plants were scorched, and they withered
because they had no root.
7 Other seed fell among thorns, which grew
up and choked the plants, so that they did
not bear grain. 8 Still other seed fell on good
soil. It came up, grew and produced a crop,
some multiplying thirty, some sixty, some a
hundred times." 9 Then Jesus said,
"Whoever has ears to hear, let them hear."
10 When he was alone, the Twelve and the
others around him asked him about the
parables. 11 He told them, "The secret of
the kingdom of God has been given to you.
But to those on the outside everything is
said in parables 12 so that, they may be
ever seeing but never perceiving, and ever
hearing but never understanding; otherwise
they might turn and be forgiven! 13 Then
Jesus said to them, "Don't you understand
this parable? How then will you understand
any parable? 14 The farmer sows the word.
15 Some people are like seed along the
path, where the word is sown. As soon as
they hear it, Satan comes and takes away
the word that was sown in them. 16 Others,
like seed sown on rocky places, hear the
word and at once receive it with joy. 17 But
since they have no root, they last only a
short time. When trouble or persecution
comes because of the word, they quickly fall
away. 18 Still others, like seed sown among*

31

thorns, hear the word; 19 but the worries of this life, the deceitfulness of wealth and the desires for other things come in and choke the word, making it unfruitful. 20 Others, like seed sown on good soil, hear the word, accept it, and produce a crop—some thirty, some sixty, some a hundred times what was sown."

A Lamp on a Stand
21 He said to them, "Do you bring in a lamp to put it under a bowl or a bed? Instead, don't you put it on its stand? 22 For whatever is hidden is meant to be disclosed, and whatever is concealed is meant to be brought out into the open. 23 If anyone has ears to hear, let them hear."24 "Consider carefully what you hear," he continued. "With the measure you use, it will be measured to you—and even more. 25 Whoever has will be given more; whoever does not have, even what they have will be taken from them."

The Parable of the Growing Seed
26 He also said, "This is what the kingdom of God is like. A man scatters seed on the ground. 27 Night and day, whether he sleeps or gets up, the seed sprouts and grows, though he does not know how. 28 All by itself the soil produces grain—first the stalk, then the head, then the full kernel in the head. 29 As soon as the grain is ripe, he puts the sickle to it, because the harvest has come."

The Parable of the Mustard Seed
30 Again he said, "What shall we say the kingdom of God is like, or what parable

shall we use to describe it?

31 It is like a mustard seed, which is the smallest of all seeds on earth.

32 Yet when planted, it grows and becomes the largest of all garden plants, with such big branches that the birds can perch in its shade."

33 With many similar parables Jesus spoke the word to them, as much as they could understand. 34 He did not say anything to them without using a parable. But when he was alone with his own disciples, he explained everything.

Jesus Calms the Storm

35 That day when evening came, he said to his disciples, "Let us go over to the other side."

36 Leaving the crowd behind, they took him along, just as he was, in the boat. There were also other boats with him.

37 A furious squall came up, and the waves broke over the boat, so that it was nearly swamped.

38 Jesus was in the stern, sleeping on a cushion. The disciples woke him and said to him, "Teacher, don't you care if we drown?"

39 He got up, rebuked the wind and said to the waves, "Quiet! Be still!" Then the wind died down and it was completely calm.

40 He said to his disciples, "Why are you so afraid? Do you still have no faith?"

41 They were terrified and asked each other, "Who is this? Even the wind and the waves obey him!"

Understanding is the reward of faith.
Therefore, seek not to understand that thou mayest believe,
but believe that thou mayest understand.
-St. Augustine

Section 3

"Daring the soul to go farther than it can see."

Study Notes:

Grace – see page 12 Study notes

Let's Dig: (2 Corinthians 5:17)

New - kainos, kahee-nos' = of uncertain affinity; new (especially in freshness; --new.)

Creature - ktisis, ktis'-is = original formation (properly, the act; by implication, the thing, literally or figuratively):-- building, creation, creature, ordinance. ---from ktizo, ktid'-zo = (through the idea of proprietorship of the manufacturer); to fabricate, i.e. found (form originally):--create, Creator, make.

Old things - archaios, ar-khah'-yos = original or primeval:--(them of) old (time). ---from arche, ar-khay' (properly abstract) a commencement, or (concretely) chief (in various applications of order, time, place, or rank):--beginning, corner, (at the, the) first (estate), magistrate, power, principality, principle, rule. ---from archomai, **ar'-khom-ahee** = to commence (in order of time):--(rehearse from the) begin(-ning). **---from middle voice of archo, ar'-kho** *(through the implication, of precedence)* = a primary verb; to be first (in political rank or power):-- reign (rule) over.

In review of what we've discussed so far; we look at the original Greek word "grace"; its meaning describes a sense of inner knowledge within us; an inner knowledge of God's existence and the influence that it has on the heart. As we become aware and recognize this inner faith and acknowledge, we can also see the gift of joy and pleasure that it brings. There is a seemingly natural sense of wellbeing that accompanies it. Try and picture it; this measure of faith like a seed that God has planted inside of us. He put us in charge of that seed; and the growth of any resulting plant is directly due to the quality and quantity of time spent with Him and getting to know Him. As faith takes root in our lives, we can choose to help our seed grow into a beautiful, flourishing plant; or we can neglect it and let it decay and wither away. We can even deny it altogether leaving us with only our humanity and nothing more. The growth of faith is all about relationship, commitment and the understanding of who He is and who you are.

Salvation is a gift, and it is offered freely to anyone who would like to partake of it! However, sometimes we might cry tears of shame and sorrow, but miss the real meaning of pure repentance and complete acceptance of the truth in Jesus Christ. Let me explain; the Holy Spirit convicts the human spirit, making us more aware of our sin. After all, we know by nature when we have done wrong and when we recognize it within ourselves; we, like

Adam & Eve, feel shame for our "nakedness" before God, and the separation of our relationship with Him. Although it can be a humbling experience; this feeling of overwhelming guilt and shame is not, in-and-of itself, a personal acceptance of God's incredible gift of salvation. Salvation in fact requires our belief, acknowledgment, and acceptance of Jesus Christ, who He is, and what He has done for mankind. There is a change that goes on in a person's heart at the moment that they truly accept God's gift of salvation! It's like having a new lease on life. You have realized now, that you don't have to go about life on your own!

> ### 2Corinthians 5:17
> *Therefore, if any man be in Christ, he is a new creature: old things are passed away; behold, all things are become new.*

There are many "good people" in the world; but our "goodness" or "righteousness" is not the ingredient that will bring us salvation. Many that do not know God, cry out to Him in moments of great need, then turn and go their own way. When the moment of desperation has passed; they never give God another thought; until the next time they hit their head against the proverbial rock!

The Holy Spirit convicts the hearts of men in hope that they will turn their heart to God and repent. God desires that we all accept His gift of grace and salvation. However, too many times the outcry for mercy and forgiveness, seems only to release the pressure of the conviction, and sadly a surrendering to Christ is not in the plan. It is definitely not through our own goodness or righteousness that we are offered and able to receive the gift of salvation; but through our repentant spirit and our acceptance of Jesus Christ as our sacrificial offering before God!

Study Notes:

Are passed away - parerchomai, par-er'-khom-ahee = to come near or aside, i.e. to approach (arrive), go by (or away), (figuratively) perish or neglect, (causative) avert:--come (forth), go, pass (away, by, over), past, transgress.

All Things - pas, pas = including all the forms of declension; apparently a primary word; all, any, every, the whole:--all (manner of, means), alway(-s), any (one), X daily, + ever, every (one, way), as many as, + no(-thing), X thoroughly, whatsoever, whole, whosoever.

Are Become - ginomai, ghin'-om-ahee = a prolongation and middle voice form of a primary verb; to cause to be ("gen"-erate), i.e. (reflexively) to become (come into being), used with great latitude (literal, figurative, intensive, etc.):--arise, be assembled, be(-come, -fall, -have self), be brought (to pass), (be) come (to pass), continue, be divided, draw, be ended, fall, be finished, follow, be found, be fulfilled, + God forbid, grow, happen, have, be kept, be made, be married, be ordained to be, partake, pass, be performed, be published, require, seem, be showed, X soon as it was, sound, be taken, be turned, use, wax, will, would, be wrought.

36

Salvation is not a dumping station for us to dump our guilt so that we can feel better and then carry on through life as usual. Christ shed His life's blood on the cross and surrendered Himself to be our sacrificial Lamb so that <u>we can</u> find forgiveness in God the Father through Jesus.

When you ask God to forgive you of your sin and contrary ways and you ask Him to come and be the Lord of your life; you are opening a door of communication between yourself and God that wasn't there before. So, you see, salvation is so much more than just feelings of guilt and cries for forgiveness; it's about relationship and friendship with our creator!

> ### Philippians 2:12 & 13
> *Wherefore, my beloved, as ye have always obeyed, not as in my presence only, but now much more in my absence, work out your own salvation with fear and trembling. **13)** For it is God which worketh in you <u>both to will and to do</u> of his good pleasure. See 2Co 3:5; Heb 13:21*

Regardless of whether you have surrendered your heart to God already or if you are still in contemplation about it, please stay with me as we dig deeper; there is so much to learn!

Salvation **is** a gift, however in accepting that gift we also accept the responsibility of caring for it. "Caring for it", you say? When you come to the point of truth and you ask Jesus to come into your heart to be your Lord and Savior, this is potentially the beginning of a beautiful lifelong relationship while on earth and throughout eternity! But, I say <u>potentially</u>, because all relationships have to be nurtured in order to really *be* an actual relationship.

Study Notes:

Let's Dig: (Phillipians 2:12 & 13)

Obeyed - hupakouo, hoop-ak-oo'-o =
to hear under (as a subordinate), i.e. to listen attentively; by implication, to heed or conform to a command or authority:-- hearken, be obedient to, obey.

Work out - katergazomai, kat-er-gad'-zom-ahee =
to work fully, i.e. accomplish; by implication, to finish, fashion:--cause, to (deed), perform, work (out).

Salvation - soteria, so-tay-ree'-ah =
feminine of a derivative of soter, so-tare' (= a deliverer, i.e. God or Christ:--saviour as (properly, abstract) noun); rescue or safety (physically or morally):-- deliver, health, salvation, save, saving.

Fear - phobos, fob'-os =
from a primary phebomai (to be put in fear); alarm or fright:--be afraid, + exceedingly, fear, terror.

Trembling - **tromos, trom'-os**= a "trembling", i.e. quaking with fear:--+ tremble(ing).

Worketh - energeo, en-erg-eh'-o = to be active, efficient:--do, (be) effectual (fervent), be mighty in, shew forth self, work (effectually in).

We have acquaintance with virtual strangers as well as some that we would call "friend". However, not all hold what could really be called a "relationship". Think about it.

When you first surrendered yourself to God and confessed your sin, you asked Jesus to come and *be the Lord of your life;* didn't you? Yet, sometimes we get caught up in the cares of this life and forget to let Him lead. We choose to go our own way, hoping or even trusting that He will follow, just in case we need His assistance. Yet the farther we travel down our own road the more we can sense the distance between the Lord and ourselves. If we desire to be led, then we must first be a good follower.

Studying God's word and spending time with Him in prayer are two major ways that we nurture our relationship with Him and learn how to follow and not stray off onto our own path so easily. In other words, stay in contact and get to know Him. As we get to know Him and His nature, we find it easier to believe and our faith naturally grows. As we grow in faith, one thing becomes quite apparent:

How we pray and what position <u>faith</u> holds in our prayer, can make a very big difference in the results that we experience.

> ### James 5:16b says
> *"The effectual fervent prayer of a righteous man availeth much."*

Look a bit harder at the "powerful" descriptions of these words. An "effectual fervent" prayer is where one is:

- **Active** - not sitting in the sidelines but active in their position.

Study Notes:

Let's Dig: (James 5:16b)

Effectual Fervent - energeo, en-erg-eh'-o = to be active, efficient: be mighty in, shew forth self, work (effectually in). From the word energes, en-er-gace' = active, operative: --effectual, powerful.

--Righteous man - dikaios, dik'-ah-yos = equitable (in character or act); by implication, innocent, holy (absolutely or relatively):-- just

--Availeth - ischuo, is-khoo'-o = to have (or exercise) force, ability, might(-ily), power, strength.

- **Efficient** - what do you think of when you think of this word? The words that cross my mind are organized, enthusiastic, detailed, ambitious, well ordered, precise, specific, clear, and perhaps even energetic.
- **Mighty in** - strong and ready to stand against any opposition.
- **Being Selfless** - laying yourself open before God, withholding nothing, hiding and covering up nothing. Total honesty, revealing your desires, motives, intentions, etc.

Romans 3:3

For what if some did not believe? Shall their unbelief make the faith of God without effect?...

Of course not! God is who He is, whether people choose to believe in Him or not. God's answer to prayer is not dependent on the belief of all those who pray, hear or are aware of the prayer. Nor is God limited by the "holiness" of the person praying. But, there is incredible, miraculous, honor and strength in the prayer that is offered through unwavering faith and pure trust!

It is not about our righteousness, but about His righteousness, Who He is and our willingness to put our trust in Him!

2 Timothy 2:11 - 15

*This is a faithful saying: For if we died with Him, we shall also live with Him. 12) If we endure, we shall also reign with Him. If we deny Him, He also will deny us. 13) **If we are faithless, He remains faithful; He cannot deny Himself.** 14) Remind them of these*

Let's Dig: (Romans 3:3)

Faith - pistis, pis'-tis = persuasion, i.e. credence; moral conviction, especially reliance upon Christ for salvation; abstractly, constancy in such profession; by extension, the system of religious (Gospel) truth itself:--assurance, belief, believe, faith, fidelity.

Effect - katargeo, kat-arg-eh'-o to be (render) entirely idle (useless), literally or figuratively:--abolish, cease, cumber, deliver, destroy, do away, become (make) of no (none, without) effect, fail, loose, bring (come) to nought, put away (down), vanish away, make void.

39

things, charging them before the Lord not to strive about words to no profit, to the ruin of the hearers. 15) Be diligent to present yourself approved to God, a worker who does not need to be ashamed, rightly dividing the word of truth.

Hebrews 10:23
23) Let us hold fast the confession of our hope without wavering, for He who promised is faithful.

"The confession of our hope without wavering"! So, if we say we believe and we have no hope, what is it that we "believe" in?

Romans 8:5-6
5 Those who live according to the flesh have their minds set on what the flesh desires; but those who live in accordance with the Spirit have their minds set on what the Spirit desires. 6 The mind governed by the flesh is death, but the mind governed by the Spirit is life and peace.

Romans 4:1-8, 13-14 (TLB)
Abraham was, humanly speaking, the founder of our Jewish nation. What did he discover about being made right with God? 2If his good deeds had made him acceptable to God, he would have had something to boast about. But that was not God's way. 3For the Scriptures tell us, "Abraham believed God, and God counted him as righteous because of his faith."[a]

4When people work, their wages are not a gift, but something they have earned. 5But people are counted as righteous, not because

of their work, but because of their faith in
God who forgives sinners. 6David also spoke
of this when he described the happiness of
those who are declared righteous without
working for it:

7"Oh, what joy for those whose disobedience
is forgiven, whose sins are put out of sight.
8Yes, what joy for those
  whose record the LORD has
  cleared of sin."

13Clearly, God's promise to give the whole
earth to Abraham and his descendants was
based not on his obedience to God's law, but
on a right relationship with God that comes
by faith. 14If God's promise is only for those
who obey the law, then faith is not necessary,
and the promise is pointless

I entitled this section "Daring the Soul to go Farther
than it can see; because if our faith only extends as
far as we can see, then we could be in serious
trouble!

I Dare you to take a stand and let go of your desire
to control your situation! I dare you to completely
and unwaveringly, hand it over to God and test His
faithfulness and care! I dare you to turn your worry
into praise, turn your doubt into thankfulness, and
turn your sorrow into joy by lifting your heart and
your hands to God saying, "I give it all to you God,
and will carry it myself no longer! I will trust you
and not be doubtful and afraid! When the thoughts
of concern and doubt come, I will refuse to take it up
again, instead I will push it away, into your capable
hands and, offer to you my praise Lord with a
thankful heart, knowing that you are in control of it
and it is being taken care of ! *Amen and Amen!*

NO MATTER THE CIRCUMSTANCES!

It is a choice and God is faithful!
Can you do it?
Yes, you know you can!

Will you do it? ....

I dare you!

Section 4
"Getting in-Formation"

In Hebrews 4:16 - it says,
Let us therefore come boldly unto the throne of grace that we may obtain mercy and find grace to help in time of need.

In taking on a bold personification, some individuals tend to assume a cocky, bossy, self-assured, and/or even a self-righteous attitude & demeanor. However, that kind of "boldness" is not expressed with a loving, respectful and humble spirit either toward God or toward man. It brings no honor before God.

God is our creator; our heavenly Father and He loves us purely and unconditionally. However, concerning being bold with God, we're talking about the assurance of knowing *who you are in Him and even more, who He is, regardless!* It's about knowing Him well enough to fully recognize Him as your Heavenly Father; and in that, approaching Him with your need in confidence that He is ready and willing to meet that need according to what He knows is best and right. It's about having the confidence in your relationship with Him to know that you can come and express your need to Him, clearly and boldly; speaking to Him with confidence and trust, knowing that you are His child. You can trust in His love and understanding nature and you don't have to be perfect in order to do so! He's perfect and that's all that matters!

Ephesians 2:18
For through him we both have access by one Spirit unto the Father

Let's Dig:
(Hebrews 4:16)

Boldly is made of two words
-1) <meta> = met-ah'= a primary preposition; properly, denoting accompaniment; "amid"

-2) <parrhesia> = par-rhay-see'-ah all out-spokenness, i.e. frankness, bluntness, publicity; by implication, assurance:-- bold (X -ly, -ness, -ness of speech), confidence, X freely, X openly, X plainly (-ness).

Grace - charis, khar'-ece = graciousness (as gratifying), of manner or act (abstract or concrete; literal, figurative or spiritual; especially the divine influence upon the heart, and its reflection in the life; including gratitude):--acceptable, benefit, favour, gift, grace(- ious), joy, liberality, pleasure, thank(-s, -worthy).

---From chairo, khah'-ee-ro = a primary verb; to be "cheer"ful, i.e. calmly happy or well-off; impersonally, especially as salutation (on meeting or parting), be well:-- farewell, be glad, God speed, greeting, hall, joy(-fully), rejoice.

That - hina, hin'-ah = in order that (denoting the purpose or the result):-- albeit, because, to the intent (that), lest, so as, (so) that, (for) to.

...

43

Ephesians 3:12
In whom we have boldness and access with confidence by the faith of him.

* Please take a few moments and read completely, the following section for deeper understanding.

Hebrews 10:19-23
19 Having therefore, brethren, boldness to enter into the holiest by the blood of Jesus, 20) By a new and living way, which he hath consecrated for us, through the veil, that is to say, his flesh; 21) And having an high priest over the house of God;
22) Let us draw near with a true heart in full assurance of faith, having our hearts sprinkled from an evil conscience, and our bodies washed with pure water. 23) Let us hold fast the profession of our faith without wavering; (for he is faithful that promised)

I've struggled, agonized and labored within, so many times with situations in my life until I got so beaten down that I could hardly see which way was up. Yet, the entire time the Lord kept saying, *"Come unto me, all ye that labour and are heavy laden, and I will give you rest. - Matthew 11:28"*

When you truly consider it, doesn't that promise sound refreshing? It sure does to me. Fact is; it sounds a whole lot better than constantly wrestling with the misery of doubt and frustration.

Remembering a period of time in my life where I felt that I had hit rock bottom in my faith. Due to discouragements brought about by well-meaning but misguided church leaders, I felt hopeless! We left the church and in all my frustration and hurt I knelt

Let's Dig:
...
Obtain - lambano, lamban'-o = a prolonged form of a primary verb, which is use only as an alternate in certain tenses; to take (in very many applications, literally and figuratively (properly objective or active, to get hold of;):--accept, + be amazed, assay, attain, bring, X when I call, catch, come on (X unto), + forget, have, hold, obtain, receive (X after), take (away, up).

Mercy - eleos, el'-eh-os = of uncertain affinity; compassion (human or divine, especially active):-- (+ tender) mercy.

Help - boetheia, bo-ay'-thi-ah = aid; specially, a rope or chain for frapping a vessel:--help.

Time of need - eukairos, yoo'-kahee-ros = well-timed, i.e. opportune:--convenient, in time of need.

before God and said to Him: "You said that your yoke if easy and your burden is light, yet this Christian walk is the hardest thing I have ever done, I was happier in the world!" "God, I'm not sure I even believe in you. If you are there, you're going to have to show me!"

I had felt so trampled down and felt like, if what I had experienced and witnessed over the previous 9 years was what it took to gain His favor, I wanted to go back to living without Him in my life! But, God is truly so good, and He heard me loud and clear! I opened my bible randomly asking that He show Himself and the scripture that stared back at me was similar to other promises, but this was for my heart alone as it said: "The Lord says to you: I will take vengeance upon those that say unto thee, 'lay prostrate that I may walk on thee'." Later I could not find that exact scripture again! But I knew in my heart that God had promised that He would take care of the oppressors and I need not feel angry and beaten down anymore! Well the Lord knew He had my ear at that point and he spoke so clearly to my heart: "Be assured, My Yoke IS easy, and My Burden IS light, however, if the yoke you are walking is too hard and the burden you carry is to heavy, then it is not my yoke you are walking, and it is not my burden that you carry! Selah

Those sweet moments with God gave me the courage and confidence to continue on and let Him guide me through to trust Him and learn to always lean on Him first. From there God led us to a Church called Happy Church, where God blessed me beyond words! Wally and Marilyn Hickey were the Pastoral leaders. I did not know who Marilyn was beyond those walls at first. Nor did I understand, what significance her words had for me that first morning until much later. We were led somehow to Happy

45

Church and into a Sunday School class that Marilyn Study Notes:
was teaching that morning. She stood in front of the
class and said: "For you that know me, you know
that I always try my best to follow God's lead,
right?" (much nodding and positive response
followed) Then Marilyn continued: "Well as many
of you are aware, I was scheduled to begin a
speaking tour this weekend, but God seems to have
other plans. He has spoken to my heart that for some
reason I am to be here teaching this class every
Sunday for a while. I don't know for how long or
why, but I want to be obedient to His will always and
so I will be here every week until He gives me the
go to move on." Over the next about 6 weeks, God
spoke to my heart through Marilyn's teachings all of
the love and grace that I needed to hear for the
healing of my spirit and the renewing of my faith! It
was primarily a pastor's wife that had nearly
destroyed my relationship with God and God used a
pastor's wife to bring me through! God is so good!

Sometimes, Christian believers in their own zeal and
well-meaning way push others to follow their lead
instead of the Lord's. Because of the appearance of
their seemingly close relationship with God or their
position and charisma, we want to trust that they are
right, but, if that burden is heavy or the walk is
drudgery we must take a step back and recalculate
and turn to the one and only leading force that keep
us on the right journeys pathway, Jesus!

But, apparently the Lord likes boldness in our faith
because He finds wishy-washiness (aka: lukewarm)
very unpalatable. He appreciates and honors
boldness and enthusiastic trust from us. Honesty and
straight forwardness is something He can work
with…. I can relate to that! Can't you?

Revelation 3:16

The Lord says: "So then because thou art lukewarm, and neither cold nor hot, I will spue thee out of my mouth."

So, if God appreciates and respects prayer that comes boldly with a humble heart, it appears that is the way it ought to be. Do you agree? Let's work on it together! Here we go...

Mark 11:24 *states,*

"Therefore, I say unto you, what things soever ye desire, when ye pray, <u>believe</u> that ye receive them, <u>and ye shall have them</u>."

God expects us to *believe* when we pray and not doubt in our hearts. How? He said that if we believe first, then...the signs of his faithfulness would follow. Those things that we need from Him will indeed follow if we only put our trust in Him.

Mark 16:17

And *these signs shall **follow** them that **believe**;* In my name shall they cast out devils; they shall speak with new tongues; ...

He didn't say for us to go do the work of the Lord and our belief will follow; he said believe (FIRST) and the power of God will follow. You can be assured that your faith will increase as you go about the Lord's work, trusting and believing in Him and witnessing His hand move!

James 2:14-26

14 What does it profit, my brethren, if someone says he has faith but does not have works? Can faith save him?
15 If a brother or sister is naked and destitute of daily food,

47

16 and one of you says to them, "Depart in peace, be warmed and filled," but you do not give them the things which are needed for the body, what does it profit?
17 Thus also faith by itself, if it does not have works, is dead.
18 But someone will say, "You have faith, and I have works." Show me your faith without your works, and I will show you my faith by my works. 19 You believe that there is one God. You do well. Even the demons believe—and tremble! 20 But do you want to know, O foolish man, that faith without works is dead?
21 Was not Abraham our father justified by works when he offered Isaac his son on the altar?
22 Do you see that faith was working together with his works, and by works faith was made perfect?
23 And the Scripture was fulfilled which says, "Abraham believed God, and it was accounted to him for righteousness." And he was called the friend of God.
24 You see then that a man is justified by works, and not by faith only.
25 Likewise, was not Rahab the harlot also justified by works when she received the messengers and sent them out another way?
26 For as the body without the spirit is dead, so faith without works is dead also. (NKJV)

Study Notes:

Note:

Genesis 15:6 (NKJV)
6 And he believed in the Lord, and He accounted it to him for righteousness.

Let's Dig:
Vs 2:20
Dead = Useless

So now if you will, please ponder the following heart examination points for a moment. This is not a test, only some thoughts for you to ponder, a self-assessment and examination, if you will:

- *How is it that I find it easy to believe in Him for salvation; but still struggle to take a spiritual stand against the things that stand in my way?*
- *Do I expect to have the power of God at work in my daily life? Am I willing to trust in that power? Think about it!*
- *Do I find it easier, to believe in the wiles (lies) of the devil than to trust and believe in the power of God?*
- *Am I sure I understand how it fits that we wrestle daily against spiritual powers of wickedness?*
- *Am I guilty of picking what portions of the Word of God I am willing to trust and believe in and dismissing those portions that challenge me to exercise my faith?*
- *How deeply rooted into God am I?*
- *How much more deeply rooted do I need to be?*
- *How deeply rooted do I want to be?*

Vigor is contagious; and whatever makes us either think or feel strongly, adds to our power and enlarges our field of action.
–Emerson

Section 5

"Strengthening Our Limbs"

I love the way my husband, expresses the condition of one's walk with the Lord;

"YOUR WALK WITH GOD CAN ONLY BE AS DEEP - AS THE WATER YOU'RE WALKING ON."

Jeremiah 17:7- 8
*Blessed is the man that **trusteth** in the LORD, and whose **hope** the LORD is. 8) For he shall be as a tree planted by the waters, and that spreadeth out her roots by the river, and shall not see when heat cometh, but her leaf shall be green; and shall not be careful in the year of drought, neither shall cease from yielding fruit.*

There is a beautiful large oak tree in town that was designated as a historical monument. One day the Lord brought Jeremiah 17:7-8 to my remembrance as He gave me a vision of that tree. He showed me visions of that tree and the experiences that a tree like this might have endured over a hundred years! I saw the tree blowing back and forth and bending unmercifully in harsh tornado winds, its leaves being ripped and torn from the branches and many of the branches breaking and flying off, only to land miles away, all mangled and torn. The Lord spoke to my heart and said, "This tree is well over a hundred years old; can you imagine what that tree has seen over all those years? Can you imagine what it has experienced?" As the vision continued I saw that tree bend unmercifully as the winds, rains and hail of

51

many a storm plummeted against it. I saw snow and
sleet piling onto its branches, as they creaked and
moaned, under the great weight of it. Some of the
weaker branches would break and fall away, and I
couldn't help but wonder how the tree itself managed
not to become uprooted and completely topple over!
I saw the earth shaking underneath it, threatening to
open wide and swallow it. I saw the heat of the
burning hot sun browning its leaves as the tree tried
to drink of the limited moisture offered during a hard
season of draught. I saw floods trying to drown it,
and insects trying to eat it away. I saw wars going
on around it, bullets ricocheting off it.   Children
climbing, putting great pressure on its branches and
scraping off the bark with their shoes. I even saw
dogs and cats doing…well, doing what dogs and cats
do to a tree! I also saw birds carefully building their
nests in it and new life being born… in that tree! The
putting up and taking down of tree houses and
families having picnics under it.   Woodpeckers
pecked at it, squirrels running up and down it and
people of all ages running circles around it. As, the
vision went on, my eyes began to fill with tears; not
only for the tree mind you, but at the realization of
the incredible message God was teaching me
through this vision:

His message was this: "The reason this tree has
continued to stand for all of these many years,
despite the many trials it endured, is because its root
system is deep and strong. As the torrents of life,
throughout the lifetime of this tree threatened to
destroy and even uproot it, it just rooted in deeper
and stronger each time and it hung on! It refused to
be uprooted; it stood tall and strong, and refused to
give up! It yielded more of its strength into its
foundation, causing the roots to grow stronger as
they rooted in deeper and deeper; all the while, its

branches continuing to reach upward continuing to give praise toward its Creator.

As the Lord continued to speak to my heart, He said, "Your God is not limited by circumstances. If you are willing to take root in me and stand strong against the storms of life; if you are willing to root in deeper, like trees do when circumstances try to shake you at the very core of your being; you will not be uprooted, and your faith and life will flourish! Come boldly before the throne of grace and let your petition be known. Leave your petition there, root in and stand strong! When the waves of doubt come in like a torrent (and they will because you're taking a stand of faith and many forces will try to derail you) stand strong and refuse to entertain those thoughts of doubt. When the waves of circumstances try to intimidate and knock you down, remember who your God is and don't look at the waves. Dig into the word and give Him your praise, keep your eyes on Jesus and trust Him for your needs, for your deliverance, even for your security and the results will be better than you could have ever imagined. *That is Faith at work!*"

So this is the formula: Speak the need, lay it down, LET GO OF IT, **trust God with it**, give thanks, and stand on that trust, …RESIST DOUBT,… continue to trust God with it, give thanks and stand on that trust … resist doubt,… continue to trust God with it, give thanks and stand on that trust … resist doubt,… continue to trust God with it, give thanks and stand on that trust …

Get the point? Every moment, every day, regardless of the circumstances, and you will have success. Praise the Lord!!

Study Notes:

Let's Dig: (Galatians 5:1)

Stand Fast - steko, stay'-ko = to be stationary, i.e. (figuratively) to persevere:--stand (fast).

Made / Free (are the same word in the Greek)- **eleutheroo, el-yoo-ther-o'-o** = to liberate, i.e. (figuratively) to exempt (from moral, ceremonial or mortal liability):--deliver, make free

Entangled - enecho, en-ekh'-o to hold in or upon, i.e. ensnare; by implication, to keep a grudge:--entangle with, have a quarrel against, urge.

Yoke - zugos, dzoo-gos' = from the root of zeugnumi (to join, especially by a "yoke"); a coupling, i.e. (figuratively) servitude (a law or obligation); also (literally) the beam of the balance (as connecting the scales):--pair of balances, yoke.

Galatians 5:1 *(KJV)*
Stand fast therefore in the liberty wherewith Christ hath made us free and be not entangled <u>again</u> *with the yoke of bondage.*

Galatians 4:8 (NIV)
Formerly, when you did not know God, you were slaves to those who by nature are not gods. 9 But now that you know God-- or rather are known by God-- how is it that you are turning back to those weak and miserable principles? Do you wish to be enslaved by them all over again?

John 8:32 (KJV)
"And you shall know the truth, and the truth shall make you free."

Mark 11:23
For verily I say unto you, that whosoever shall say unto this mountain, Be thou removed, and be thou cast into the sea; and **shall not doubt in his heart, but shall believe that those things which he saith shall come to pass;** *he shall have whatsoever he saith.*

James 4:7
Submit yourselves therefore to God. Resist the devil, and he will flee from you. (KJV)

It's pretty evident that the Lord wants us to speak to Him with a level of hope, faith, and trust already intact and activated. It's a fact that as human beings, we have no problem speaking our need to God. In fact, all too often if we don't receive the answer we are looking for or don't receive an answer in a "timely manner" we assume that God either didn't hear us; or He forgot and needs a reminder. So, we keep telling Him over and over. But, God heard you the first time, and He knows what you need better than you do. Have you considered that maybe you need to get on with the next step? ... Remember what it is? ...I'm talking about the THANKING part, the STANDING part? The PRAISE part? THE TRUSTING PART? Oh...that! Yes...that! "That" part tends to be the hardest for us. We expect to speak and instantly have what we ordered... just like at a fast food window! I know, because... well... "Been there, done that!" Until I began to get a clear understanding and recognition of Who it is that I am praying to!

When I speak to people about total trust and pure faith like this, the response I hear time and time again is something like this: "I did, but...!" "I tried, but..." I'm trying to, but..." "I do trust Him, but...

But? But what? You're concerned about...? About what? Your worried that... what? That God won't... what? Consider this pattern of thinking... is this faith or is this doubt?

Doubters invert the metaphor and insist that they need faith as big as a mountain in order to move a mustard seed.
–Anonymous

Section 6

"Beyond Doubts Shadow"

"Beyond a shadow of a doubt I know,
He hears each word I say....
There's not a thing that God cannot do for me,
I only have to pray..."

Words to a wonderful song that gives a lift to my heart every time I think of it! Is this not the major key to our faith? Beyond a shadow of a doubt... "the substance of things hoped for, the evidence of things not seen". That is the confidence that we must walk in.

God knows your need and He wants to meet it, however, He knows the perfect time and the perfect way to answer your prayer. He also desires that you have the confidence in Him; <u>without a doubt</u> that it is <u>His</u> answer that you seek; trusting that He will not fail you! He desires your answer to come at just the right time and in the right way, leaving no doubt that it was He who brought that answer. However, in this process keep in mind that, actions do most certainly, speak louder than words. God is looking for the evidence of your faith. We prove our faith by walking in it! One of the first steps toward a walk of faith is to pattern your life after the characteristics His word teaches and let His glory shine through you before the world. Consequently, we must leave our burdens at the feet of Jesus and back off from them! God waits for you to honor Him with your trust, your praise, your adoration, and your thanks for who He is, what He has done and will do for you. These are perfect moments to bring glory to God and let Him shine in your life! How will we conduct ourselves when times are tough? Will you walk in faith? Or will you exhibit your lack of faith and your

57

frustrations for the world to see. It is when you exhibit your faith and confidence, in that very same God that you confess to believe in, that you will see His faithfulness in action! As He works to meet your need, the world will stand in amazement at the awesomeness of it all!

God will not force His way into our life' situations. He gave us a free will. But, He wants an invitation and He wants us to put our trust in Him. However, too often we get so caught up struggling with our situations that we don't even try to give it to Him. Frankly, why should He bother getting involved, as long as you have control? God is not a pity party crasher! When you're ready to end the party and send all the guests home, God will be happy to help you clean up the mess. So, how about it? Let's send all those pity partiers home now! Don't invite any of them to stay! Especially those famous ones like: "Hopeless Worry", "Depresh Eon"; "Fretful Lost Lamb"; "Achy Breaky"; "Inner Turmoil"; "Resent Ment"; "Frust Raition"; "But I", Well I", "What if I", and the whole "I" family! Send them all where they belong; into the sea of forgetfulness. They do a great pity party, but… what kind of party is that…who needs it?

Now seriously, there are many ways that we demonstrate a lack of faith. For example, have you ever used the cliché'; "It's just my Luck"? If you have, or someone around you has; a common response from many a Christian is; "there's no such thing as luck".

Howbeit that their response is true; the <u>heart behind the cliché'</u> is actually <u>the **real** issue</u>. How about, "It's par for the course"? Oh my, what a hopeless statement! Cliché's like these are a symptom of a lack of faith and hope. It's a way of saying, "I'm a worm and not worthy of better." Or "I don't expect that anything should come out right for me, because I'm a goof-up"; or "Nothing ever goes right for me, so why should I expect it to now".

Oh, ye of little faith... **bite your tongue!**

When statements like these and thought processes have become a common part of one's life, it can indicate a more deep-rooted condition. We must each examine our hearts; and examine our thought processes and find where these tendencies might be stemming from. We need to surrender these issues to the Lord and allow Him to teach us a better way of thinking! Sometimes negative thought processes become habit, stemming from earlier years of poor influences or a lack of self-esteem and/or self-confidence. It may have become such a pattern of life that you may not have even recognized this issue as a problem previously. However, it is not harmless! It can hold a person back in life, and even more critical; it hinders us from becoming all we can be in our relationship with our heavenly Father! It is important that we catch ourselves in our negativity and learn to choose faith building words; words that edify the spirit and glorify God! Our words and thought processes make all the difference in whether or not we succeed in anything that we set our hearts to accomplish!

In considering our thought processes and our condition of heart, let's not forget to examine our belief standard. Quite often, the reason that we cannot seem to stop the flow of negative statements like the ones we have discussed, is that we have not changed our "belief standard". For example: If you truly believe that "bad luck" just follows you around; or that you are destined to have "bad luck"; you need to weed that kind of poisonous belief standard from your data banks!

Spending more concentrated time in prayer and study of God's word will help you to begin the process of extraction and removal. You may also consider seeking some council from others that have overcome in this area. Either way, what you're dealing with is a spiritual "cancer", and it needs to be healed! It must be replaced with a firmer relationship with Jesus, and a pure knowledge and understanding of who you are in Christ; and even more so, how much you can accomplish through Him! So; let's move along with our study so perhaps we can begin the healing processes that are needed.

Joshua 1:8
This book of the law shall not depart out of thy mouth; but thou shalt meditate therein day and night, that thou mayest observe to do according to all that is written therein: for then thou shalt make thy way prosperous, and then thou shalt have good success. (KJV)

Wow! What powerful words! Read it again carefully... the more of God's word that is planted in you the more it will come from you. Bloom where you're planted? Plant yourself in His word and see what grows!

Jesus told us, the words that proceed from our lips are extremely important to Him, in fact critical! In the book of Matthew (12:36), the Lord says, that one day we all will have to answer to Him for every <u>idle</u> word that we speak.

Let's Dig: (Matthew 12:36)

Word - rhema, hray'-mah =
an utterance (individually, collectively or specially), by implication, a matter or topic (especially of narration, command or dispute); with a negative naught whatever:--+ evil, + nothing, saying, word.

Idle - Argos, ar-gos' =
from 1 (alpha = of Hebrew origin; the first letter of the alphabet) = (as a negative particle) inactive, i.e. unemployed; (by implication) lazy, useless:--barren, idle, slow.
...

60

Matthew 12:36

But I say unto you, that every idle word that men shall speak, they shall give account thereof in the Day of Judgment. (KJV)

Whoa! Makes me want to stand up and take notice of each word coming from my mouth. In fact, without getting off track, let's take a quick look at this word, "idle", in the Greek.

As you can see; the Lord is trying to get us to understand that idle words are potentially destructive; but also, at the very least, they are non-productive and useless. Only "life giving" words of faith and trust should proceed from our mouths; instead of the useless words that tend to pass our lips so often. Critical, angry, destructive and/or other types of counter-productive words only prove to destroy our reputation as ambassadors for Christ; as well as interfering with our ability to enjoy the closer walk with Jesus that we yearn and pray for.

A number of years ago, I heard a widely respected Evangelist talking about control of the tongue and how often it is mentioned in the Bible. He said, in his research he had discovered that the word of God mentions control of the tongue more times than it does the subject of salvation! I don't remember the exact calculations that he quoted; but, no matter, because; since then, I have taken special notice of these passages as I do my studying and they truly are numerous! Kind of makes it seem important, don't you think?

The following scripture makes this point pretty clear as it describes the power in the words that we speak. The attitude that we take with our faith will reveal itself through our words. So, as we look at this, remember what I said earlier that "actions speak

Study Notes:
...

Give - apodidomi, ap-od-eed'-o-mee = to give away, i.e. up, over, back, etc. (in various applications):--deliver (again), give (again), (re-)pay(-ment be made), perform, recompense, render, requite, restore, reward, sell, yield

Account - logos, log'-os = something said (including the thought); by implication, a topic (subject of discourse), also reasoning (the mental faculty) or motive; by extension, a computation; specially, (with the article in John) the Divine Expression (i.e. Christ):--account, cause, communication, X concerning, doctrine, fame, X have to do, intent, matter, mouth, preaching, question, reason, + reckon, remove, say(-ing), shew, X speaker, speech, talk, thing, + none of these things move me, tidings, treatise, utterance, word, work.

louder than words"? Also remember that the intent of the heart is quite revealed by our choice of words!

Luke 6:43-45 (NKJV)
"For a good tree does not bear bad fruit, nor does a bad tree bear good fruit.
44 "For every tree is known by its own fruit. For men do not gather figs from thorns, nor do they gather grapes from a bramble bush.
45 "A good man out of the good treasure of his heart brings forth good; and an evil man out of the evil treasure of his heart brings forth evil. **For out of the abundance of the heart his mouth speaks.**
Also see: Mt 7:16-17, Mt 12:34-35

Now, let's not get caught up into judgmental thinking and presume that; every negative comment spoken by someone is an automatic indication of "evil" in that person's life. Do we really have reason to highly question that individual's sincerity with God? Careful, lest you take on a self-righteous, judgmental spirit! When a spiritual cancer truly does exist, it reveals itself through a consistent pattern. A single idle comment, or even a temporary pattern of negativity is also not necessarily sufficient for a "diagnosis." As we set our sights on a more "heavenly minded" existence, it is all too easy to fall into a position of judging, or stereotyping people (a very "judgmental" position). If we feel that there is a problem in someone's life, then love and grace is what will bring results and offer the "cure." Hold them up to the Lord in prayer and love them through it! Be careful, that we don't take scriptures like this and use them incorrectly. Stop and think about it; by judging others and living by the letter of the law, you put yourself in the position to be judged (yourself) by God. Be careful what kind of thoughts you entertain in your heart and your mind. Entertaining and following harsh thinking patterns fills the spirit with critical tendencies and will only lead you into judgment.

That said; let's continue on with more understanding. We've discussed what faith is and what doubt is. We have also discussed how very important it is that we understand these things clearly.

You may trust in the Lord too little, but you can never trust Him too much.
–Anonymous

Section 7

"Where the Rubber Meets the Road"

The inspiration for this book was birthed out of my experiences where the situation was totally beyond my control and I had to take a strong stand on faith and put my trust totally in God! God put it on my heart to write those testimonies down. I pray that the testimonies and learning experiences written in this book will encourage and inspire you to, taste of the Lord and see that He truly is good and faithful.

It was approximately 1990 and I had been fighting warts on my right hand for years, I tried wart removers, and even had some cut out by the doctor but those horrible warts kept coming back each time and even spreading into more. A dear friend suggested, "Why don't you rebuke those warts in the name of Jesus and command them to dry up and fall off". I said that maybe I would but whenever I considered her suggestion I struggled with so many contrary thoughts. I had thoughts like, "Is that really right for me to expect such a mundane little thing from the all-powerful God?" "Maybe I could try the wart remover again, maybe I didn't do it right… maybe God just wants me to take care of this myself somehow; after all I can't expect Him to do everything for me, can I?" and I continued to analyze and agonize: "Oh, I don't know; sounds like some of that overly emotional Holy Roller type stuff! That's just too emotional for me, I'm a realist; it just doesn't seem realistic." "don't think I could do it!" And then came: "What if I try it and it doesn't work, that would really mess with my mind and my faith; wouldn't it?" "I don't know about that idea, I know other people say they have done it, but I've never really

65

seen the evidence firsthand. Hummm?" "Seems just too weird for me…I'm just not that kind of person, I don't think I could…?" …And so, I continued on, 2 MORE YEARS talking myself out of trying to trust my situation to the Lord!

I wrestled with the warts and with my spirit, continually chiding myself for my unwillingness to take the stand of faith needed in trusting this situation to God. I just could not seem to give it to God, *silly me!* However, finally one day I really rose up in anger at the warts and at my stubborn, fearful doubt! That was when I had a serious, life changing talk with the Lord about it, *"You know something Lord, she was right; these warts do not belong on my hand. In fact, they don't belong anywhere in my life! After all, I am a child of God, the Almighty creator of heaven and earth! I do not believe that it is your will for these warts to exist in my life!"* At that point, my spirit started to rise-up in righteous (and royal) indignation and I thought, "why not?" The Lord has healed things much more complicated than this. He said in His word that we could do the same, and even more, with just a tiny little dose of faith the size of a mustard seed! Have you ever seen a mustard seed? He said for us to try him and taste of His goodness and faithfulness; so, I said "I believe it is about time that I put my trust in You for this!"

Now, mind you, it was not God's *ability* that I questioned. I questioned whether it was important enough to Him to meet the need. I also questioned whether I had any right to expect it. Thirdly, I questioned myself as to whether I had it *in-me* to trust Him for this. I realized by now, that once I made the decision to turn it over to God, there was no turning back! Anything less would mean that I failed to trust Him, and I would not have experienced

God's faithfulness in this matter. *It was time for me to take a stand!*

Psalm 34:8-9
O taste and see that the LORD is good: blessed is the man that trusteth in Him. (KJV) v.9 - O fear the LORD, ye his saints: for there is no want to them that fear him.

How I wish I could tell you that I just simply rebuked those warts in Jesus name and they instantly/miraculously disappeared. However, remember what Jesus said about asking anything in faith, believing that you *have* received! Now the question was; can I put my faith where my mouth is?

So, I told the Lord, "I know that in your word that, as a believer, I can ask you to provide for needs like this and I believe it is about time that I really trusted you for something! I ask you to forgive me for not being willing to trust you for this healing sooner. I'm so frustrated with these warts on my hand Lord! I do not believe that you would want them on my hand any more than I do; so, I'm going to put this in your hands and trust **you** to remove these warts. Lord, I know that they do not belong on my hands and I do not accept them anymore. Help me to believe and trust you for this."

At that point, the feeling that was going through me, reminded me of the comment made by #5 in the movie "Short Circuit" when he said, "Jet's, don't fail me now!" In my heart I was saying, in earnest, to Jesus, just like the man in the bible, "Lord, I believe, please help my unbelief!" *(Ref.: Mark 9:24)*

I took a deep breath (kind of like "get ready, get set, GO!), I began to speak to those warts: "Warts, you do not belong on my hand or anywhere on my body,

67

so in the name of Jesus, you dry up and fall off!" Okay, I did it!... Did they instantly fall off? No! (with a slight grin) ...it wasn't difficult to figure out where the problem was. Even I knew in my heart, that at that moment my trust just wasn't meeting my words. Oh, don't be mistaken; at that moment, my faith was definitely "standing" ...yes siree! It was standing in a corner somewhere; ... like a shy/hopeful wallflower, waiting to be asked to dance or perhaps for a command to fall in at attention! Either way, it needed some work!

At that point, knowing full well that I had not spoken those words in faith, I knew I had to try it again! I was having a real struggle between what was coming from my mouth, and the thoughts in my head. I knew I had to take a stand of infallible faith and trust; a stand that had no room for doubts and "natural reasoning" or analyzing. My heart recognized that God *was* able to do it, but this is where "the rubber meets the road" as they say. I am convinced in my heart that God is real and that He is perfectly capable of meeting my need, but I was still fearful that He might have other ideas about the warts on my hand. I feared that if I trusted Him for this and these warts were not healed, my faith would be shattered forever! I also struggled with thoughts that I might be asking for something that I shouldn't, and that perhaps this was something God just expected *me* to take care of. Whew! The battles of the mind, how troublesome they can be! (Gross understatement?)

But then I thought, "now wait a minute here, I *have* tried to take care of this and didn't get anywhere. I remembered, what Jesus taught; that we must put our trust in **Him**! Putting our trust, not in *our* own words, or in our own self-righteousness; and we most definitely have to look to **Him** for our answer; *setting aside all knowledge of the circumstances*!

68

What? You can believe in Him for grace, salvation, daily guidance, as well as, trusting Him to intervene in dire situations when we pray! Yet, you can't trust him for something as little as warts? Hummm. Are you sure about that? Those are the little foxes, spoiling the vine; those things that "so easily beset us".

So, I repeated my command to those warts, with much more determination and righteous indignation against them! And I repeated it again! And again! About ten times in all; I repeated it until I could sense that my faith began to "mustard" up! I THEN KNEW in my heart IN WHOM I BELIEVE, and **finally**, I WAS PERSUADED THAT HE IS ABLE TO KEEP THAT WHICH I HAD COMMITTED TO HIM on that day! Committed! That was a crucial key! From that moment on, I knew I had <u>committed</u> those warts to Him and *He would* take care of it!

After I took that strong, bold stand, I heard the anxious words in my mind, "Look! Look and see! Are they gone, yet?" I remembered the scripture, "Be anxious for nothing" and I knew somehow that the voice was not one I should listen to; so, I refused to look at my hand and chose to <u>just</u> plant my seed of <u>trust</u> and leave it there. I trusted that God would meet my need and He would let me know when the time was right to look at my hand. Amazingly, the rest of that day I didn't even think about it anymore, it had disappeared from my thoughts. By God's grace and mercy, I did not think about or look at my hand for nearly two weeks (as they say, "out of sight, out of mind")! I believe *that* in fact was truly God's grace at work! It was about 10 days or so later that I heard the gentle voice of the Lord saying, "look at your hand." That was the moment I remembered, and so I looked. I was so amazed that I had forgotten all about it for that period of time, yet even more amazed and grateful that: **the warts were completely gone!!!**

Study Notes:

Was it easy to take that stand; to endure; to trust without doubt? Not at first, but *once I had determined to truly and faithfully put my trust in Him and commit that whole situation to Him,* he met me there and from **that point** it was easy! You see, once I full heartedly decided to give it to Him, it ceased to be *my* problem anymore. That made it easy to forget about it and wait.

Over the next 7 to 8 years some of those warts tried to return; at least 3 separate times that I can recall! But, I took a stand again and rose up in righteous indignation against them, stood on the promises, and rebuked them! I said, "NO! No way! You do not belong here and in the name of Jesus, you dry up and disappear. I will not accept this, and by God's grace I am free of you, warts! Thank You Father, in the name of Jesus I stand, and I trust you, for **you are** faithful"; and I **refused** to **entertain** any thoughts of doubt.

Now, you might be thinking, "Wow! What a woman of faith; I could never do that." As they say: "Never say never"! Perhaps you're wondering; if I possess such great faith, does it just fall-in at attention any time I have a need? Do I easily trust God now for all my needs? Are you kidding me? To be (embarrassingly) honest…NO! ... Now, are you shocked? You can call me goofy or perhaps, just plain bull-headed! But you know something? … Although I still struggle with the, seemingly never-ending, battles of the mind that everyone experiences, ultimately, I know that God will meet my need! He can, and He will! Despite any mental battles that I face and weaknesses in my faith; God in His goodness brings His blessed faithfulness to my remembrance and that helps me to find the strength to stand and believe. When **I** grasp onto those memories, they encourage and strengthen my ability to muster up the measure of faith that I need to trust again!

Faith is kept alive in us, and gathers strength,
more from practice than from speculations.
–Addison

Section 8
The Last Resort?

It's hard to grow your faith
inside of your comfort zone!

"You may go through difficulty, hardship, or trial – but as long as you are anchored to Him,
you will have hope."—Charles Stanley

> **Psalms 71:3** *(NKJV)*
> *Be my strong refuge, to which I may resort continually; You have given the commandment to save me, for You are my rock and my fortress.*

> **Proverbs 15:4**
> *A wholesome tongue is a tree of life, but perverseness in it breaks the spirit.*

> **Proverbs 15:23**
> *A man has joy by the answer of his mouth, and a word spoken in due season, how good it is!*

There are many things that we, as believers, say and do that work against our ability to trust in God. Let's take a look at some of them. See how many of these points seem familiar:

I remember one day when my conscience, seemingly smacked me upside the head with the proverbial 2x4! It brought to my attention a comment I had just made (a very common comment, even among Christian believers). I had been going through some very hard struggles in my life and felt like I had tried everything I could to find a remedy. I knew all along, and all too well, that this situation was not within my own control, but I kept trying anyway! Later while complaining to a friend, she suggested that I just needed to pray; to which I responded:

> "I guess there's nothing else I <u>can</u> do but pray and trust God!"

Suddenly, at that very moment I sensed in my spirit the Lord's disappointment. It was as if He had thrown His hands up in the air, and cried out, "What am I, chopped liver?" I cringed and mentally popped myself aside my cheek as I suddenly realized how much my comment had just devalued God and His love and faithfulness! I began to examine the reality of how often we put God in the position of the "last resort"! "Oh, Dear God, forgive me", I said.

So often we speak of our problems to God, asking Him for help; but do we ever, <u>really ever,</u> honestly trust Him to do so? Do we trust while taking a step back; and <u>watching,</u> <u>expectantly</u> for His answer? As human beings, we tend to hold onto the defeating idea that we must have full control of our situations. We feel that we must have complete understanding of the whole situation before we can trust it into God's hands. So therefore, we fear that letting go of that control (even to God) might let the problem go unattended and unmanaged or even perhaps mismanaged. What does this really mean? In this case, although it is likely unintentional, we have doubt as to whether He can or will meet our need!

So, our tendency then, is to lean on our own understanding, our own ability, and our own strengths to get us through. This kind of thinking is more within our comfort zone, or seemingly! You might think: "Well I just need to figure it out." I guess there is some comfort in that, huh? I think that sometimes we assume that because we spoke and cried out to God about our need, it's automatically in His hands. But; then we continue to worry and fret about it and try to manipulate the situations surrounding it. Finally, when we feel that nothing is working (including God); we turn again to Him in exasperation, or maybe even anger and blame Him for allowing the situation to go on! We still don't recognize that we never really trusted the situation into His capable hands in the first place! Ask yourself this; "have I ever really managed to completely, unreservedly trust Him? I mean handing it over to Him and letting it go? Fully choosing to trust that He can and will take care of it? Please understand this: you may have believed the entire time that He is capable. But, what is it that really hinders you from choosing to believe that He will? What stops you from letting go of control in order to just "simply" trust God?

Open your heart right now and be totally honest with yourself; let's look at some of the possible problem areas, ok? First and foremost, we must examine your belief standard. Initially I might ask; do you struggle with inner doubts of God's real existence? If so, consider going back to some basics and take some time out to get yourself acquainted with Him and who He is. Take some time and read the book of John (even if you have before) and ask God to help you to discover who He is through those scriptures. Maybe like me, you feel pretty confident in your salvation, but you struggle with thoughts of doubt about God's willingness to meet the particular need that is before you. Perhaps you're caught up in the circumstances and you just have a struggle with

75

letting go of "control"? Regardless of what it is that hinders you remember this: "if the burden is still a burden to you, then you have not let it go!" Fact is; the reason why it is such an issue is because it is probably outside of your control or even completely out of control and only God has the power to "fix it"? Whatever it is that hinders you from placing your complete trust and unfaltering faith in God Almighty at this moment, is what will continuously hold you back from realizing His power and glory at work in your life until you surrender it!

One of the most common thought patterns or concerns is: "What if God doesn't meet my need?" "What if His answer does not come when I need it; or not be what I expect it to be when it comes? I'm afraid that it might shake any confidence that I have in Him already and hinder my ability to trust in Him ever again!" Wow! That is a Biggie! I fought that Stinkin' thinkin' for two years concerning the warts on my hand!

Not to belabor it but, perhaps you're not sure how to recognize God's answer when it comes. Maybe you're afraid to trust Him for fear that it might not be the answer that you want. Etcetera, Etcetera! There are so many excuses to not step out in faith! Can you see the vicious defeating pattern of carnal thought here? This is why I express whole-heartedly to anyone that wants to understand this equation: "Faith is a <u>complete</u> and <u>solid</u> (unwavering) <u>Trust</u>"! "It is a personal choice!" Balancing your faith on the fence post of the "what if's" is missing a very essential ingredient... Trust!

We used to have a dog named Skeeter. That dog loved climbing the fence into the neighbor's yard but had been firmly disciplined for doing it many times! He became more and more sneaky about it, although

76

he knew that it was wrong! He was a Lab/Shepherd mix and was a fairly large dog. One day as I looked out into the yard, I caught him as he reached the top of the chain-linked fence! When I yelled out the door at him, he froze atop the fence, perched like a bird (mind you he did not jump the fence, he always climbed it)! As he teetered atop that fence to consider his options, he finally lost his balance and fell clumsily into the neighbor's yard. He tucked his tail and hung his head in shame, knowing full well that he was in trouble! I struggled to keep a stern composure because of the humor of it all, but he had to learn! After all that discipline and care, he still didn't trust me enough to believe that going into that yard was a bad idea. I won't go into detail, but his obsession with that neighbor's yard cost him and our family dearly later!

Are you teetering atop the fence, not sure how to trust God and His wisdom, or whether you should try? Are you more inclined to keep relying on your own thoughts, strengths, ability, and/or desires? Do you talk yourself out of it before you begin?

When we first meet someone, the natural flow as human beings is to place a small measure of our trust in that new "friend". If all goes well; then as we get to know that person better, our trust begins to grow, and their trust in us as well! And so, it is the same with our relationship with God. The better we know Him, the easier it is to trust Him! The more your relationship grows between you and God, the more God can also trust you.

Our dog Skeeter didn't have the same reasoning power that we are capable of. He only knew what he wanted! What was really best for him was not as important to him because, <u>he was determined to control his situation</u>!

77

You can see God's power and grace all around you; but, when you place your complete trust in Him, you will than begin to taste and see of His goodness on a personal level. The more you place your trust in Him, the more your relationship with Him will grow, and your faith will begin to rise into higher heights than you can even imagine!

> **Nahum 1:7,**
> *"The LORD is good, A stronghold in the day of trouble; and He knows those who trust in Him."*

God knows whether we trust Him or not, He knows every innermost part of our being and knows your heart better than you ever will! He wants to meet your needs and for you to grow in His wisdom and knowledge. Part of that growth experience is learning to cast your burdens on Him. I'm talking about the "stumbling blocks" dealt to us in this life for whatever reason and by whatever means; He tells us to cast all of those cares upon Him!

<<*Just a small Dig:*
(Nahum 1:7)

This word
trust = chacah, khaw-saw' *comes from a primitive root; meaning to flee for protection; and figuratively, to confide in:--have hope, make refuge, (put) trust.*

Think about it!

78

Worrying doesn't change anything,
but trusting in God changes everything!
– Christian quote

Don't be afraid, just believe!
– Mark 5:36

Section 9

Casting Is Only Part

For with God nothing shall be impossible.
                                    Luke 1:37

While pondering and studying the word "Cast" as found in Psalm 55:22 many thoughts came to mind. One train of thought was of my wonderful nephew "TC", the great outdoorsman. He absolutely loves to hunt and fish! In fact, for a time he worked for a resort in beautiful Aspen, Colorado teaching vacationers to fish, in particularly to fly fish. He enjoyed it for a time, but personal fishing was where the real joy was. Sometimes turning a hobby into work can rob you of the joy of the hobby!

Anyway, one thing that I found interesting about him is that when he is highly stressed he literally "goes fishing"! It's how he releases tension and thinks best through his situation. I thought actually, it makes perfect sense! Considering that fishing truly is a relaxing sport; and can even be a bit rewarding if all goes well! As I continued on this journey of thought; I pictured him in my mind casting his line and waiting; but, then it hit me! A fisherman slowly reels his line back in! When the line is left to set for a period of time without moving along through the water, it is more likely to get caught up into plants and things at the bottom of the lake. Are you catching the application of thought here? Let's continue…

Although I have never watched him Fly fish, I am told that it is one of his specialties. I got to thinking about the method of fly fishing. I imagined him casting out his line and just as it would seem to

80

lightly kiss the surface of the water; he would quickly pull it back, just to cast it out again and repeat the scenario over and over again! TC would probably wrinkle up his nose and get that notorious grin of merciful pity at my non-expert's description of it all, but basically; it is a fair enough view of the event.

Considering all of this, sent my head and heart spinning with such incredible new understanding of this idea of "casting our cares"!

> Psalms 55:22
> Cast thy burden upon the LORD, and he shall sustain thee: he shall never suffer the righteous to be moved. {burden: or, gift}

The typical thought process of this "Casting your burdens" on the Lord is commonly related to fishing, but perhaps it should be more commonly likened to "casting" or "throwing" a rock into the sea? Let's discuss for a moment, another all too common viewpoint and perhaps some fresh thought for your consideration.

Picture for a moment a fisherman casting his line out into the water. He hopes to reel in something good but; of course, has no idea for sure if he'll catch anything. So, he patiently waits with hopeful expectations.

Within this line of thinking, consider that, when you cast your cares and burdens to God something special happens; in return, He casts His line to you. It's a line that can draw you into His love, joy and grace-filled peace and presence. But if you still have hold of your fishing rod, fishing anxiously for answers, your hands won't be free to grab hold of <u>His</u> line. In other words, when we cast our burdens

to God we must leave them there, out in the sea,
letting go completely.   It is *no longer yours*!
Actually, the "casting" here in
Psalms 55 is talking about "casting" or "throwing"
your cares as you would a rock. Imagine it this way:
take your burden, wrap it around the rock, throw it
out to Him, let go and forget it! Why would you
even want to dangle those burdens on a line? They
will just pull you down... or possibly even crawl
back up the line like a big hairy spider! Who needs
it! Don't even skim that rock on the water, don't
belabor it; just toss it out there to the Lord; you can
trust Him with it!

What's that? Did I hear you say, you've tried giving
it to God? Let me ask you this; "then why are you
still holding onto it?" You say you're just not sure
how to?" Well... you can't very well hand your
burden over to the Lord, while your polishing it with
your doubt and fear! "What are you going to do with
it? If you keep casting it out and reeling it back... If
you keep it dangling from your line while you hold
onto it at the other end... it's going to come back
with all kinds of mucky debris like worry, doubt and
frustration! What good is that?" Burdens tend to
become heavier with time. Wait a minute! Did I just
hear somebody say, "I gave it to God; but it's just
too hard?" or... I think somebody else said; "God
hasn't answered yet and I have to do... **something**!...
I can't just sit here and wait!" Oh really? But, if
you've already scrubbed it over and over and it still
comes out even more stained and dirty, what makes
you think scrubbing it yet again will improve it?
Throw it away!!!

There are all kind of analogies, but back to fishing.
To my knowledge, when casting a line from a fishing
pole, the "normal' tendency is to eventually reel it
back in; correct? Well, imagine this: Burdens make

for a very heavy bait; so, you can guarantee that they will drag the bottom as they are reeled back in. They are going to come back coated with all manner of dirt and debris, seaweed, and slimy residue; which makes the burden even heavier, dirtier, and really smelly. Now the burden is heavier and full of things that will not only weigh you down but, cause you to "stink" lower into your situation. (That was not a typo!) Quick! Cut the line!!!

So, in retrospect, what is this debris, seaweed and so forth? It is in fact; the negative circumstances and the impatience, worries, and doubts that you dragged it through as you were reeling it back in. When you cast your burden to God, this is not a line you should ever care to pull back. Again, burdens are heavy, like rocks; cast it out to God like a rock, and let it go! If it seems to sink to the bottom where you can't keep an eye on it any longer... GOOD! It belongs to God now and is no longer your concern. So, now you can allow yourself to go searching for that wonderful and desirable safety line that God casts out to anyone who will look for it. It is baited with pure "agape" love and coated with the wherewithal to stand strong against the waves. Perhaps He'll even teach you how to "walk on water" if you will just hold tight and keep your eyes on Him!

The Sea of Forgiveness and Surrender, the Sea of Forgetting and of Mercy; these are names for some of the swimming holes where you can find that line of safety. We are not the ones that need to be fishing out there for relief of our burdens! Jesus is the master fisherman and He has a fishing line that can hold any amount of weight. He also owns the sea and can control all of its elements. Once you cast a burden into that sea it belongs to Him and He is in control of it. There's one hitch though... He gives YOU a choice; you have the right and ability to either leave the burdens in His care, or, you can reel them back or dive in and gather them! Your choice! Who is doing the fishing today?

In summary; trade in your pole and fishing line for a rock. Wrap it tightly with your burden. Throw your rock in and seek for His line. It's not hard to find. Grab onto His line and taste of His bait! After all, YOU are what He is out there fishing for! Oh, to be Jesus' catch of the day! Every day!

Proverbs 30:5
Every word of God is pure: he is a shield unto them that put their trust in him. {pure: Heb. purified}

James 1:3
Knowing this, that the trying of your faith worketh patience. See Ro 5:3

Trying of my faith? I always thought that this word "trying" meant harsh trials and hard times. Yet, when I got my eyes off of myself and looked again, I saw that what God is telling us, that as we prove His (God's) faithfulness, by trusting in it; our faith will be increased! This is not about putting us through trials. It is about refining our faith through our testing, trying and tasting of God's goodness! We will go through trials; that is a given. But these trials are grand opportunities to get to know God better! And what's more, we will grow and be strengthened in our own faith by giving God opportunities to prove Himself and His faithfulness to us.

Study Notes:

Let's Dig: (James 1:3)
Trying = dokimion, dok-im'-ee= *-on -a testing; by implication, trustworthiness:--trial, trustiness:--experience (-riment), proof, trial.*

Faith = pis'-tis = *persuasion, i.e. credence; moral conviction (of religious truth, or the truthfulness of God or a religious teacher), especially reliance upon Christ for salvation; abstractly, constancy in such profession; by extension, the system of religious (Gospel) truth itself:-- assurance, belief, believe, faith, fidelity.*

Patience = hupomone, hoop-om-on-ay' *- cheerful (or hopeful) endurance, constancy:- enduring, patient continuance (waiting).*

84

When life becomes all snarled up,
offer it to our Lord and let Him untie the knots.
–Book of Days for Christians

Section 10

What are you waiting for?

The morning is crisp, the day is long;
the dusk of night brings peaceful song,
The rooster crows it's evening call,
the crickets play their song to all

As sun has set the moon will rise,
and stars will shine in midnight skies
The birds and trees have stood the test,
all of nature is ready for rest

Oh, son of man, look 'round and see,
what wise rewards do wait for thee
Stand strong and await, for God is there,
to guide you through with loving care!
                                          – Lu Scrogan

Psalm 34:8
O taste and see that the LORD is good:
blessed is the man that trusteth in him. (KJV)

God's children are hesitant to ask God for patience. Rumor has it that when you pray for patience you will experience trials! You know something? You might be right! However, we should not fear the process; because after all, patience is developed through trials and difficult experiences and we need not fear. Recognize also that trials and difficulties are part of the life package; so, the trials that seem to suddenly appear after we ask for patience are not necessarily a result from that request! We may have just connected them because of the timing! Either way we can be confident that God is our deliverer and present help in times of trouble!

Although it is true that trials help us to learn patience; consider for a moment that it is not the only

86

way for us to develop patience! The most productive way to develop a patient heart and spirit is to test God's faithfulness by choosing to put our complete trust in Him! Placing your need into His hands, walking by faith, not by sight, taking a firm stand against all doubt and fear! That is what increases our faith, and in-that also increases our willingness and ability to be patient. Patience is a product of faith, impatience is a product of doubt and fear. The more you put faith to the test, the more your faith grows!

With our daughter and grandchildren living with us it can surely put our patience bones to the test! It can also, exercise their ability to endure and be patient with us! Some mornings I am called upon to be the school taxi driver and although it can try my patience, I realize that getting my feathers ruffled over it, just makes me lose feathers!

A better way to look at it, is that it gets my day moving a bit sooner and I'm able to get my time with the Lord in earlier and proceed from there into what can become a more productive day! Turning the would be "curses" into blessings! Imagine that… exercising a positive mindset can do wonders for setting your spirit free!

Another lesson that I have learned is, rather than ask for patience, I personally prefer to ask God for strength, endurance (emotional, mental, and/or physical) and wisdom. Asking Him for the wherewithal to help me to stand against fear, doubt and circumstance can sometimes be quite similar to asking for patience; but, it helps me to carry on with more stamina and more careful thought. I encourage you to ask for the strength to endure so that you will not crumble under the weight of the problems that you face. Ask Him, to speak to you continually, His words of encouragement are wise reminders of the

Study Notes:

promise of victory! Rely on Him for the strength to hang on, so that you can succeed in this goal to increase your faith. As you choose to put your trust in Him, faith will grow, and patience will be obtained. Just remember again: *Impatience* is a byproduct of a lack of trust and faith.

John 14:13
And whatsoever ye shall ask in my name, that will I do, that the Father may be glorified in the Son.

Psalm 91:1
He that dwelleth in the secret place of the most High shall abide under the shadow of the Almighty.

Psalm 91:2
I will say of the LORD, He is my refuge and my fortress: my God; in him will I trust.

We *must* go to God with our desires and our needs and at the same time, recognizing that *He is God! He is* the one that carries all wisdom, knowledge and authoritative power! Being confident in that fact, we can also be confident that he knows what the best remedy is for our need. Trust *Him* to decide how the need must be met and in what manner, what time, where, and through whatever means.

I am reminded of a situation years ago, when a friend of mine had discovered that she was pregnant with her third child. She already had two boys and upon the news of this third pregnancy she set her heart firmly on trusting God for a girl this time. She prayed, and prayed, and went to friends at church and had them pray over her as well.

When she told me that she had asked God for a girl and she was "<u>standing on faith</u>" and trusting for it, she said, "after all God said that He would give us the desires of our heart, didn't He?" Seeing, that she had given God this ultimatum, I felt it important to ask her if she might consider, even if for just a moment, the possibility that God might have a different plan for her life and the life of the child she was carrying? This was not intended to raise doubt or thwart her desire to take a stand of faith in this matter. However, it was intended to help her see and understand that ultimately it is God's will that we must seek, not our own, and that our stand of faith must be in balance with His will. Always leaving the ultimate outcome in His capable hands! She was adamant and was refusing to even discuss anything else! I pleaded with her, "please, just humor me for a moment and consider this simple question... What if God wants to give you another boy?" I could barely get the words out of my mouth before she adamantly and stubbornly refused to even entertain the idea and said that it would be a lack of faith to do so! She cried out to all who would hear her for their support of this stand. Unfortunately, as a result of her strong determination and outcry, there were several well-meaning Christian friends, through a heart of compassion, "prophesied" over her that she would in fact, have the girl that she desired". This of course fired her up even more! (Note, that we as Christians must be careful what we speak over each other's lives. In well-meaning moments, we can miss God and lend our support to something that we should not!)

Well, you might have guessed it!... When the baby was born, it was... in fact... another boy. She blamed her husband and yelled at him in the delivery room for his lack of faith because; during the pregnancy, the father of the child had refused to limit

God, and said that it wasn't important to him what gender the baby was. He said that he was just praying for a healthy baby!

It is not for us to tell God what the outcome will be, it is only for us to bring our petitions, our desires and our needs before Him and let Him have full control of the outcome! He knows what we need before we even ask, but He will not force His way into our lives; we must invite Him into the situation with our trust and faith.

Does any of this contradict what we've already discussed about standing and trusting God in faith? Absolutely not! But if we are to learn to walk in faith, we must also learn that in everything, we must first allow God to **be** the ultimate decision maker! He knows what is best. He knows who, what, when, why, where and how!

James 4:3

Ye ask, and receive not, because ye ask amiss, that ye may consume it upon your lusts. {Lusts: or, pleasures} (KJV)

Yes, with God all things are possible; however, not all things that we ask are in balance with God's will and desire for us. Can you see what the problem was with this young woman's stand on faith? We know that her desire to have a daughter was not evil. However, she was allowing the desire of her own heart to consume her to the degree that she was not willing to consider that God may have a different plan for this child and her family. She stood on scriptures that promised that if you seek God, He will give you the desires of your heart. But perhaps she forgot to consider the wisdom in the first few words of Psalm 37:4, "Delight yourself in the Lord and He will give you...". If we ask only out of our own desire and we do not seek to align it with His, we

Let's Dig: (James 4:3)

--Amiss - kakos, kak-oce' = *badly (physically or morally):--amiss, diseased, evil, grievously, miserably, sick, sore.* <u>From the word</u> *--kakos, kak-os'* = *apparently a primary word; worthless (intrinsically), i.e. (subjectively) depraved, or (objectively) injurious:-- bad, evil, harm, ill, noisome, wicked.*

might ultimately find that His desire differs from ours. She had refused to remember that God is the giver of life and her husband's desires would no more override God's plan than hers would! It was ultimately God's plan that this child was a boy and only God knew why.

As life went on, I am not aware of what happened ultimately to this young couple and their three boys; but, God has His hand on them and I know that they desired God's will for their lives. So, my prayer for them has been, that they could find it in their hearts to let God teach them through this experience and help them to grow spiritually and emotionally so that they might raise these boys in the love, joy, and wisdom of God. The boys would be grown now, and I would love to discover one day that this boy had become a great God-fearing leader. But either way, I have continued to bring them up before my Heavenly Father as they have crossed my mind continually throughout the years! My desire for this precious family has been faith, joy, prosperity and Godly wisdom in abundance for them all!

We must always remember that God knows you better than you could ever know yourself. He knows your abilities, your strengths and your weaknesses. The trust that you place in Him must be firmly planted in your spirit along with the conscious and clear acknowledgement that His wisdom is sufficient. Not giving Him the answer that **you** think you need, but just placing your need before **Him**, setting it down and **leaving it** in His capable hands.

When we decide to put our trust in God for something, we have to keep in mind who **He** really is! He is not some magic Genie that fulfills wishes. He is our Heavenly Father; our parent and creator that desires to help us learn and grow. What He wants most is for you to become the person that He created you to be. Perhaps that third son of this young woman was destined to be the next "Billy Graham" or Abraham Lincoln of sorts?

Whatever we ask God for; we must remember that God looks at the heart and at the need. He knows what your motivation is, what your reason is, and He already knows the details before you ask. Most of all, He knows what is right and what is best for you and for your specific situation. So, if you ask, you can be assured that *He will* answer. However, first you need to be prepared to wait for His answer, however long it takes. In addition, and just as important; you must be ready and willing to accept the answer that He gives! It's all part of that complete trust.

Let's go on:

> ***Psalm 1:1***
> *Blessed is the man that walketh not in the counsel of the ungodly, or standeth in the way of sinners, nor sitteth in the seat of the scornful. {ungodly: or, wicked}*
> ***Vs.** 2 But his delight is in the law of the LORD; and in his law doth he meditate day and night.*
> ***Vs. 3 And he shall be like a tree planted by the rivers of water, that bringeth forth his fruit in his season; his leaf also shall not wither; and whatsoever he doeth shall prosper.***

While considering the fact that plants and trees have built in instinct to root in deeper upon a threat of uproot; can you see the wonderful correlation that God has offered to us here in nature? As we are thrust into trials and tribulations, unlike the trees, we have a tendency to allow damage of uprooting occur. We focus on the problems instead of the solutions and the blessings that are there for us!

God created us and blessed us with all that we need to survive this war called Life! There are many survival tips even found in God's creations to help us if we will just take a look! Many are spoken of in His word. Read, study, ponder, look around and take a deep breath… breathe in His goodness and count your blessings! Stand on his word and promises and Trust!

Study Notes:

Look at that beautiful butterfly and learn from it to trust in God.
One might wonder where it could live in tempestuous nights,
in the whirlwind, or in the stormy day;
but I have noticed it is safe and dry under the broad leaf
while rivers have been flooded and
the mountain oaks torn up from their roots.
– J. Taylor

Section 11

Where is de-Light!

Psalm 37:4-8
4.Delight yourself in the LORD and he will give you the desires of your heart. 5.Commit your way to the LORD; trust in him and he will do this: 6.He will make your righteousness shine like the dawn, the justice of your cause like the noonday sun. 7.Be still before the LORD and wait patiently for him; do not fret when men succeed in their ways, when they carry out their wicked schemes. 8.Refrain from anger and turn from wrath; do not fret—it leads only to evil.

What better teacher of Faith than what we can learn by stepping out of our comfort zone and choosing to stand against doubt and fear and Trust the Lord.

God blessed us with one daughter, who we dedicated to God by faith, as a small baby. She has been a blessing to our lives in so many ways; but, as things go, as parents we have had some times of trial as well.

At a time when our daughter was dating this particular young man, we knew without a doubt that he was totally wrong for her. In fact, they were both wrong for each other. They brought out the worst in each other. During this relationship, she began to rebel like never before and we had many serious concerns about where she was headed and even for her future happiness. We had become extremely concerned that she might run off and marry this young man! They both sensed that we did not approve of the relationship although we purposed to never treat him with distain or rudeness because, the harder we tried to get her to see the problems in this

95

relationship the tighter she clung to him (an all too common reaction in these kind of circumstances). She was convinced that we were just being judgmental and unfair and even accused us of being rude to him!

I was nearly to the point of a nervous breakdown with worry and concern when the Lord began to get through to me:

> **Matthew 6:25**
> *"Therefore, I say to you, do not worry about your life, what you will eat or what you will drink; nor about your body, what you will put on. Is not life more than food and the body more than clothing?*

I began to realize that we had not been trusting in God for our daughter's welfare; but living in constant worry. She was my only daughter and I was too emotionally involved and kept ignoring and sidestepping the very One that could actually do something to help!

Short detour:
Please excuse this little detour but, before I finish this stroll down memory lane, let's take a moment and examine some of the sights along this road.

> ### *Philippians 4:6-8*
> *Be careful for nothing; but in everything by prayer and supplication with thanksgiving let your requests be made known unto God*
> *vs. 7 And the peace of God, **which passeth all understanding**, shall keep your hearts and minds through Christ Jesus.*
> *vs. 8 Finally, brethren, whatsoever things are true, whatsoever things are honest, whatsoever things are just, whatsoever*

Study Notes:

Let's Dig: (Philippians 4:6)

*--**Careful** <merimnao> = to be anxious about :--(be, have) care (-ful), take thought; solicitude:-care.*

*--**Supplication** <deesis> = a petition:--prayer, request*

*--**Thanksgiving** <eucharistia> = gratitude; actively, grateful language (to God, as an act of worship):- - thankfulness, (giving of) thanks (-giving)*

96

things are pure, whatsoever things are lovely, whatsoever things are of good report; if there be any virtue, and if there be any praise, think on these things. {honest: or, venerable}

God brings me to verse 8 often! He takes me there, so my thought processes can be dissected or purged, and I can get some healthy perspective. I like to call this scripture: **"God's measuring stick."**

Remember what we said earlier about casting our burdens? In 1 Peter chapter 5, Peter spoke another message about something that we must cast out to God; "our care". Are we talking about burdens again? No, actually in this case it is so much more!

Read on and Dig.

1 Peter 5:7-11
Casting all your care upon him; for he careth for you.
***vs. 8** Be sober, be vigilant; because your adversary the devil, as a roaring lion, walketh about, seeking whom he may devour:*
***vs. 9** Whom resist steadfast in the faith, knowing that the same afflictions are accomplished in your brethren that are in the world.*
***vs. 10** But the God of all grace, who hath called us unto his eternal glory by Christ Jesus, after that ye have suffered a while, make you perfect, stablish, strengthen, settle you.*

Here's where we STAND:
Not only standing on the promises in tough times but also looking to the building of our

Let's Dig:

(1 Peter 5:7-11)

*--**care** = merimna, mer'-im-nah (through the idea of distraction); solicitude: -- care.*

Webster's definition:
Solicitude - so·lic·i·tude
n.
1. The state of being solicitous; care or concern, as for the well-being of another. See Synonyms at anxiety.
2. A cause of anxiety or concern. Often used in the plural.

Vs. 9
*--**resist** = anthistemi, (anth-is'-tay-mee) **to stand against, i.e. oppose:-- resist, withstand.***

97

relationship with the Lord! We must give God our devotion and all of the glory, even in the midst of adversity. ...

And finally:
> *vs. 11 To him be glory and dominion for ever and ever. Amen.*

This phrase, "casting your care" *(vs. 7)* is talking about your focus *on Him*, your love *for Him*, your devotion *to Him*; and even your concern *for Him*. Caring about His desires and needs! Wow, did you ever stop to concern yourself about God's needs? What does God need? He wants to taste of our compassion for His desire. He desires to see the evidence that we care about Him and our relationship with Him. Being a friend to someone means that you show that you care about their feelings, goals, and desires. ***Even when that friend is God!*** This scripture passage in First Peter is not meant to make you focus on *you* and *your* needs, but it's about how to focus and rely on *Him*! Besides, giving Him your cares and trust can be quite rewarding! What a concept! Casting not just your problems onto him, but your loving encouragement, your praises and even your thanks *for* Him as well! We must not forget that God put man on this earth for companionship!

Matthew 6:33 & 34
> *"But seek **first** the kingdom of God and His righteousness, and all these things shall be added to you.*

Let's face it! We not only struggle against giving Him control; we, tend to make it all about ourselves. We tend to forget about the close friendship/kinship that we are meant to have with God. In your thought processes, is He so regal that you struggle to really

Let's Dig:

(Matthew 6:33)

First = proton, pro'-ton = *firstly (in time, place, order, or importance):-- before, **at the beginning**, **chiefly** (at, at the) first (of all).*

Righteousness - dikaiosune, dik-ah-yos-oo'-nay = *equity (of character or act); specially (Christian) justification:-- righteousness.*

98

believe that this God that you cannot see with your eyes honestly desires friendship? Even better, a close family relationship with you? A caring Father or Brother that is willing to see your problem as worthy of His time?

Study Notes:

We say we believe (in theory), but when push comes to shove, we tend to trust God only when it comes easy. When things are either going well and you perceive your needs as few or minor, do you give much thought to this friend? On the other side of the coin, when you've hit total rock bottom and He's your only hope, what do you tend to do? Oh, how often do we try to convince ourselves that we *are* putting things in God's hands, although we haven't really trusted Him with much of anything yet? When was the last time you laid your cares at the feet of Jesus and truly LEFT THEM THERE? All the while, standing firmly, lifting your praise and refusing to falter, or to be uprooted, just like the tree planted by the living water? In that also, letting loose of all the threads of worry, doubt, concern, control and really letting him hold it all?

> *vs. 34* *"Therefore do not worry about tomorrow, for tomorrow will worry about its own things. Sufficient for the day is its own trouble. (NKJV)*

In other words, taking each day, one day at a time, (like TODAY), while allowing and trusting God to bring you through and meet you in every situation!

Ending detour!

Taking all of this into consideration, let's move on.

As I said: I began to realize that we had not been trusting in God for our daughter's welfare but living in constant worry. I realized that I was driving myself into a frenzy over this relationship my daughter was in, and not really trusting God at all! Please don't get me wrong; I *was* praying and asking just like we all do! Asking over and over; with my heart full of much worry and fret. I felt I had to do something! As I kept searching frantically for what it could be that I could do to get her to see the problem! I was angry and wanted to control the situation! Obviously, I had not really committed her to God yet; and not worked at all to really trust her and her life into His capable hands!

At the point of that realization, I got angry at the devil and at my own foolishness; I rose up in righteous indignation and realized that although it was not within *my* power to change this situation; it is well within God's ability! My power existed only in my ability to let go and let God take control, putting my complete trust in Him.

At that point, I spoke out in boldness and I said to God, "God I realize that there is nothing more *I* can do about this situation; but, I know *You* can. Anything *I* do only drives her deeper into this relationship. Lord, I know that this relationship is not what you would desire for her and I know that you have a better plan!"

100

This is where the determination and the commitment to stand, really started kicking in, I got angry at the situation and so desired God's will to be at work in it. So, (in righteous indignation); I put aside all doubt and fear and took a strong stance of spiritual rightness and faith from deep within my spirit! I spoke this to the Lord:

"She is our only child Lord, and **I DID NOT GIVE BIRTH TO THIS CHILD TO SEE HER RUIN HER LIFE BY MARRYING A MAN THAT WOULD BE SO WRONG FOR HER!** A man that would eventually crush her spirit and drive her farther from all that she can be in you, Father! **God, we dedicated her to you as a baby, and I <u>here and now</u>** trust her into your capable hands... again! I give her totally to you and trust **You** to take care of this situation in her life, **<u>I know You can and I know You will</u>**! Lord help me to continue to trust and stay out of Your way. I want her to become what *You* would have her to be, and I thank You, for your love and mercy; God, you are so faithful. Praise Your Holy name!"

Well, I must say, it felt rather good to let it go and hand it over to God! At that point, I knew what I **must** do; I needed to back off! Every day was a challenge, and sometimes every moment was a challenge. After all, this was my only child, and I had been through months of fear that this man would influence her to run off somewhere and marry him.

Mind you, it was not that this young man was some evil monster; there was no good to be seen in this relationship, present or future. It was crystal clear that this relationship would only lead to unhappiness and problems in the future, yet she was too caught up into it to see.

Now, very important... after I committed the situation to God, I knew that each day would be a challenge and I had to purpose in my heart to *stay out of it*! I began to identify with Paul where he said, "I die daily", referring to the daily crucifying of the flesh. However, I also knew that I must not dwell on my concerns, worries, anger, fear or frustrations; I just needed to put my eyes on Jesus and trust it all into His capable hands.

Please note that this doesn't mean that I sat and cried and whined to God. That kind of action would be an act of doubt, and in-that abandoning my stand of faith! I just continued to remind myself that it was not my problem anymore! It was being taken care of and I had to root in deeper and support the stand I had taken! I continually lifted my praises to the Lord and thanked Him for what He had done, what He will do, and especially for WHO HE IS!

Well, of course, God *is* faithful...did you ever doubt it? Within a couple of days, she and this young man were discovering many conflicts in their relationship. They began arguing constantly and she was beginning to see that she could not marry him. She finally realized that it was not a healthy relationship. Within two weeks from the time that I committed her into God's hands, she put an end to the relationship and it was over!

If I asked you, "Did you trust this need to the Lord?" What would be your first response? Just a short review:

Would it sound something like this?
- "Well, I did, but it is so hard!"
- "I tried to <u>but</u> _____" (you fill in the blank)
- Yes, I have, and I keep asking Him... <u>but</u> _____"
- "All I *Can* do is trust the Lord!"

- "I keep giving it to Him, <u>but</u> nothing changes!"
- "I have been, <u>but</u> I can't just wait, I have to do something!"
- "It's just not that easy!"
- "Yeah, I do trust Him, <u>but</u> _____."

Hebrews 11:6
But without faith it is impossible to please him: for he that cometh to God must believe that he is, and that he is a rewarder of them that diligently seek him.

Next Question:
"When in the midst of trial and tribulations, **Is God greater than your circumstance?**" "…then this situation?"

Here and now you might say "Oh yes, of course He is, God is greater than any circumstance!" And that answer would be correct. But do you really, unreservedly believe it? When asked this question, in the midst of trial, typical responses are things like… (you fill in the blank)

- "Well, Yes but" _____

- "I guess, but _____"

- "I don't know because I don't know enough about _____ (referring to the situation)"
-

Who's in control of this need? Where is your delight found?

Study Notes:

103

Walk into de-Light and you will find it is very clear and bright! You will find that God truly is greater!! A play on words? Yes and No, because He is the Light that gives guidance through the dark, narrow pathway and He is also our source of delight and joy! So, life is a journey and he knows all of the best hiking trails!

Psalm 3: 3-8

3 Let not mercy and truth forsake you: bind them about your neck; write them on the table of your heart: 4 So shall you find favor and good understanding in the sight of God and man. 5 Trust in the LORD with all your heart; and lean not to your own understanding. 6 In all your ways acknowledge him, and he shall direct your paths. 7 Be not wise in your own eyes: fear the LORD and depart from evil. 8 It shall be health to your navel, and marrow to your bones.

Want to be healthy? Learn to give it all to God! It's a healthy experience and good for your body as well as your soul!

Remember that "Insanity is doing the same thing, in the same way, time after time, year after year expecting new and better results!"

But,

Delight in the Lord... and follow His lead! He's is in charge of the lantern and He knows when and where to light the path!

*Our Confidence in Christ does not make us lazy,
negligent or careless, but on the contrary, it awakens us,
urges us on, and makes us active in living
righteous lives and doing good.
There is no self-confidence to compare with this.
– Ulrich Zwingli*

Section 12

When We Stand in de-Light!

I John 1:6 *(NIV)*
If we claim to have fellowship with him and yet walk in the darkness, we lie and do not live out the truth.

I pray that the testimonies shared in this book will serve as reminders of God's love and faithfulness; and trust that the thoughts and encouragement shared in this work will be a source of inspiration and encouragement. That it can be used to help anyone that desires to grow in their ability to trust God and to build a growing relationship with Him. May it be a source of strength along life's journey to serve as a source of reminders and guidance in trusting Him to take care of those things that would try to grip one's life and stand in the way of a victorious walk with God.

I've searched my heart and looked over my life. What I see is that too many times I have allowed the opinion and attitudes of society; as well as my own perception of the same, to detour or hold me back from what I could have been accomplishing; and in fact, even block my ability to trust God completely. I have, in fact, allowed myself; as well as my own lack of self-esteem and self-confidence, to join in the battle against me! The battles of the mind are a constant weapon that the enemy uses (quite effectively, I might add) to keep us off balance! He does it because it tends to be so effective! Daily study in God's word and keeping the communication lines open between you and God through prayer are

106

the greatest weapons we have, to win the battles...
and the war!

In I Thessalonians 5:17 the Lord tells us to pray
unceasingly. Obviously, it doesn't mean that we
should spend our whole life physically down on our
knees in prayer? I believe what the Lord is trying to
teach us, is that we should be in constant, continual
spiritual communication with God, in our hearts, our
minds, and our spirit. Staying mindful of God's
presence and communing with Him, as a constant
companion. An accountability partner, a shopping
companion, a car passenger to commune with, etc.
This is critical! He is with us all the time, throughout
our day! Why don't we talk with him? He's not
going to just sit in your prayer closet like a doll on a
shelf, waiting for you to show up; although at times,
He is treated as if He is! Sometimes He is treated like
He like He is a genie in a bottle! Think about it!
Where did you "leave" him last before you set him
aside in your mind and went on with your day? Don't
go looking because He's just a call away! Just call
out to the Lord and He is there!

I have learned that when I talk with Him throughout
my day. He is a great help and communicator! When
I shop I like to ask for His wisdom, His opinion, His
help. Not because I'm afraid of making my own
decisions, but rather to seek His wisdom. We don't
need to fear making a move without divine
inspiration from God; but to keep Him close and
keeping your spirit tuned to His Spirit allows you to
learn of His wisdom and builds your relationship
with him; not to mention, it can help save you from
making costly mistakes! Not everything we do
requires divine inspiration but seeking and then
following His wisdom can help you to make the
wiser decisions and save you a lot of grief.
Additionally, when your spirit is tuned in to His

107

presence you are much more aware of your own attitude and behavior which helps us to present ourselves in a better light before those that do not know the Lord and are searching. Being more aware of the conviction and guidance from the Holy Spirit helps one to keep our own spirit tuned up! I personally find that when I follow this pattern, I am usually quickly aware of His presence and I tend to instinctively give Him my repentance and my attention immediately and work to focus my thoughts on those things that I should.

I love to discuss my joys with Him, my frustrations, my decisions, worries, anger, etc. He is such a comfort, especially when I am perplexed with a decision. Whether to speak or not speak; how to approach a subject or if to approach; and even in the seemingly small things: which one to buy or not buy; whether to go or not go and so on. However, there are those days when life has me overwhelmed and rather self-absorbed. It is then that I am tempted to hide myself (like Adam & Eve did) and do my own thing, as I throw "caution to the wind". So, I try to run away and hide from Him, or ignore His presence. Sometimes we fool ourselves into "thinking" that perhaps "distractions" will be a good excuse! Well, obviously, at those moments we're really not **thinking** clearly at all; you do remember who He is... right?! (Grin!) Excuses do not work! Quick repentance will work if it is genuine! However, clear honest communication is what brings us closer to Him.

Sometimes the desire to give into temptation and follow our own reckless thinking is so strong and hard to resist! Instead of seeking the Holy Spirit's wisdom and guidance, we forge on ahead; sometimes making very serious errors that can lead us to reaping very difficult and even disheartening consequences. In all reality, at times it can seem easier to ignore His presence and just do your own thing and deal with the consequences later, right?

In the early 1980's, we had a business that we ran from our home! When my husband started the business, it was truly Godly inspired! It grew fairly fast and provided very comfortably. We continued to trust the Lord, ask for His guidance, pay our tithes and involve ourselves in whatever the Lord lead us to and life was good! Any financial expert will tell you that most businesses work in the red for the first 5 years or so before they show a profit! The business we had, did not show a loss from day one! It was amazing!

However, after a couple of years, we began to feel a bit cramped in our little house and decided that perhaps we should consider selling and moving to a larger house. All in all, the idea was fine, we prayed at the start that God would guide and lead us to the right house; to "Open doors where they need to be opened and to close the doors that need to be closed!"
However, month after month, our house was not selling although we found a house that we decided to buy! We put a contract on it, with a contingency on the sale of our house, <u>but we forgot to pray first</u>! More time went by and it came time for them to break the ground for the foundation on the new house. They called us and said that if we still wanted the house, we needed to sign a form that would cancel the contingency and commit us to the purchase whether our house sold or not! We again did not take the time to discuss it with God in prayer or search our hearts for His peace; we just decided to do it! Our realtor said to go ahead and sign it and if necessary, last minute, he would buy our house, so we could get our closing done and then buy it back

from him right after. We assumed that the house would sell before long, it was a great buy! You guessed it! It came time for our closing and our house was still not sold!

God is good though, because despite our foolishness, last minute our buyer appeared! Our realtor still had to do the same deal and on the same day of our closing on the new house, but we got through it! However, that was the beginning of the end of things as they were! It not a wise plan and definitely not God's plan!

The buyer for our house had surfaced just in time to make our plan with the realtor work, however; the first month of business in the new home showed our first month of loss since the beginning! Within 5 years we had to file bankruptcy! We lost our business, our home (and all of the equity from our first home that went into it) our pop-up camping trailer that we dearly loved and so much more. Additionally, God moved us halfway across the United States to Georgia! We had some hard lessons to learn!

The primary lesson here was that we had asked Got to open doors that needed to be opened and to close doors where they needed to be closed! Looking back, we see that God had tried to close the door on that house by ours not selling and the builder insisting on the removal of contingency! But, we were not staying vigilant in keeping our ears and hearts tuned to the Lord's voice and the guidance of the Holy Spirit! We just slammed that door wide open by signing that removal of contingency! It was God's mercy that the sale of our sweet little house sold on the same day as our closing on the new one! But, our actions brought us consequences that we would not have suffered, had we kept our focus on the Lord and His wisdom!

God has been good and gracious to us and has blessed us over and over in so many ways since then! He brought good out of what had gone wrong because he cares for us and is a very loving Father! We learned many things from that experience and continue to learn more as we commit our lives to Him as well as the lessons learned when our own desires get the best of us!

Have *you* ever found yourself assuming that you don't need the help of the Holy Spirit, just to fall on your keister later? He expects us to use the mind that he gave us to make decisions for our lives. However, if your spirit is tuned-in to Him (despite how good you think your decision is); you can save yourself a lot of trial. Have you ever just felt a deep feeling within of unrest; or a strong struggle with indecisiveness about something? At that point, it would be a most critical time to pay attention and follow His lead!

At times, I admit that I have just let myself get absorbed with life all around me and forgotten that He might actually have something to offer to my day! Something more than just watching me making decisions and struggling through my mistakes.

He loves to offer guidance and see us succeed! With all of the stresses of life, He is so often, the very source of the joy that helps to keep a song in my heart as I encounter the dreaded, yet inevitable, inconveniences and ugly situations throughout my day. He really is the best friend you can hang out with, and He doesn't mind if you have other friends along; as long as you don't ignore Him! If I walk in faith, trusting in Him fully for all of my needs, my relationship with Him will be firm and strong. The closer I am to Him the easier it is. You can truly trust Him!

Matthew 5:14-16

14Do everything without complaining or arguing, 15 so that you may be blameless and pure, children of God without fault in a crooked and perverse generation, in which you shine as lights in the world 16as you hold forth the word of life, in order that I may boast on the day of Christ that I did not run or labor in vain.

I will sing of His love forever!

Psalm 89:15 (NLT)

Happy are those who hear the joyful call to worship, for they will walk in the light of your presence, LORD.

Peer beyond the wall of doubt to embrace the possibilities
--Truth

"*He is no fool who gives what he cannot keep,*
to gain what he cannot lose."
-Jim Eliott

Section 13

An Inch of Trust Measures Many Miles

Luke 6:38 *(NIV)*
Give, and it will be given to you. A good measure, pressed down, shaken together and running over, will be poured into your lap. For with the measure you use, it will be measured to you."

When I first married my husband, I naturally invested a measure of my trust in him. This trust was a little stronger of course, than the measure of trust that you would usually offer a new friend. Naturally, as our marriage grew, and I came to know him better, I learned to trust him more. My trust in him continued to grow year after year as I got to know him better and gain the confidence that I could literally and fully trust him with my life!

That kind of trust is how God wants you to trust Him and even more! He *is* the friend that sticks closer than a brother! Closer than a parent or a spouse, in fact, closer and more trustworthy than anyone! He gave His life and shed His blood for you! Who can you trust more than that?

Ask yourself the following question: "What is standing in my way?" "Why do I find it so hard to trust Him", or "Why do I struggle and resist handing myself and my situation over to Him?" Take a break now, to look at your situations and meditate on your answers.
Pick one of your situations and test the waters! Exercise your Faith and see that the Lord is good!

Sometimes you just have to jump in to see that the water is fine!

First part of this exercise:
Totally commit and affirm that,

> **2 Timothy 1:12**
> *"...nevertheless, I am not ashamed: for I know whom I have believed and am persuaded that **He is able to keep that which I have committed unto him** against that day."*

Second part of a good spiritual workout!
To start the test and then take a taste:

> **I Peter 4:19** *(NIV)*
> *So then, those who suffer according to God's will should commit themselves to their faithful Creator and continue to do good.*

> **Psalm 34:8**
> *O taste and see that the LORD is good; blessed is the man that trusted in Him.*

> **I Peter 2:1-10**
> *Therefore, rid yourselves of all malice and all deceit, hypocrisy, envy, and slander of every kind. 2 Like newborn babies, crave pure spiritual milk, so that by it you may grow up in your salvation, 3 now that you have tasted that the Lord is good.*

> **The Living Stone and a Chosen People**
> *4 As you come to him, the living Stone— rejected by humans but chosen by God and precious to him—*
> *5 you also, like living stones, are being built*

115

into a spiritual house to be a holy priesthood, offering spiritual sacrifices acceptable to God through Jesus Christ.

6 For in Scripture it says:

> *"See, I lay a stone in Zion,*
> *a chosen and precious cornerstone,*
> **and the one who trusts in him**
> **will never be put to shame."**

7 Now to you who believe, this stone is precious. But to those who do not believe, "The stone the builders rejected has become the cornerstone,"8 and, "A stone that causes people to stumble and a rock that makes them fall." They stumble because they disobey the message—which is also what they were destined for. 9 But you are a chosen people, a royal priesthood, a holy nation, God's special possession, that you may declare the praises of him who called you out of darkness into his wonderful light. 10 Once you were not a people, but now you are the people of God; once you had not received mercy, but now you have received mercy.

Study Notes:

Cornerstone - The cornerstone (or foundation stone) concept is derived from the first stone set in the construction of a masonry foundation, important since all other stones will be set in reference to this stone, thus determining the position of the entire structure.

Related Words: Anchorage, brace, bulwark, framework, infrastructure, substructure, support, premiss, backbone, nucleus, seat, soul, touchstone...

He is our Cornerstone: our hope, our foundation, our anchor, our backbone, or lighthouse! He is the one in whom we can trust and lean on!

Despite all our weaknesses and failings, God is so good; yet, we so easily forget! This is why God laid it on my heart to do this study and to share with you some of the wonderful things that He has done in my life. If prayer were a building structure, belief and trust would be cornerstones. Because without *belief*, prayer is just empty words and without substance. Belief without *trust*, is very shaky ground and will likely crumble at the first challenge! You see, remember that even Satan and all of his angels believe...

> *James 2:19 (NLT)*
> *You say you have faith, for you believe that there is one God. Good for you! Even the demons believe this, and they tremble in terror.*

...and they tremble because they know who He is and what they are and what will become of them!

Belief is real, but if there is no trust in it, then it is only an acknowledgment of fact and not real Faith! Faith has substance, it has hope, it is an action, an exercise, not merely an acknowledgment of the facts! It requires a measure of trust in order to become: FAITH!

Again, I trust that the depths that God has taken us through in His word will prove to edify you, as much or more as it has edified me!

So now, I'm going to take a couple of moments to jot down a couple more of those testimonials of God's faithfulness.

I'm reminded of the time when our daughter was about 2 years old and Ken was out of a job. I will not say that he was out of "work", because being out

of a job and being totally out of work is not one in the same. Sometimes doors opened for extra work that helped to supplement a little, although a job position for consistent income had not shown itself yet. However, it took over 8 months, with very little money coming in, for him to find a consistent job position. To this day we cannot explain, how our bills managed to get paid! But we do know that during that time we were faithful to worship and go to God's house; but more importantly, <u>we</u> faithfully <u>tithed</u> on any and <u>all</u> monies that came to us and continued watering our souls with His word and putting our trust in Him! You might wonder if we lived off credit cards or an excess of generosity from others. When I think back to that time, I am so excited, and I rejoice to be able to say unequivocally, **NO**! We did not use credit cards or have to rely on the generosity of others! We were so blessed to see the hand of God work in our lives, and it was simply miraculous! Like I said, we can't explain how we managed to make it through, other than it was God's blessing and we are truly thankful!
We trusted **God, and He was Faithful!**

There was another time that Ken was out of work in the mid 1990's, for about 1½ years! The company he had been with had to close its doors. He was able to do some commission work with his former boss, but; there were many weeks where we saw the bills coming in and we had no money. However, we had taken a stand to trust in God. We continued to tithe on whatever money we received. That was our first priority! All the while, we prayed while we determinedly refused to entertain thoughts of doubt and fear! Bless God! Somehow, the bills were always paid! Remember, this went on for 1½ years! We Trusted **God and He showed us that He is truly Faithful!**

I'm reminded of the story of Jacob in the bible where his father in-law had hired him to take care of some of his sheep. His father in-law's intention was to pay Jacob as little as he could get away with. So, he determined that he would pay Jacob with speckled sheep from the flock; which were much less desirable sheep. Talking about getting the short end of the deal, huh?

Well regardless of his father-in-law's selfish greed, Jacob was a Godly man and gave God thanks for whatever he received. Interestingly, God saw to it then, that most of his father-in-law's sheep began to give birth to speckled sheep and Jacob's sheep gave birth to the more desirable sheep! So, Jacob was very blessed because he trusted God! (Who says God doesn't have a sense of humor!)

You see; God honored my husband and I, because we purposed in our hearts to do our best to be faithful to Him. It's easy to believe and worship when things are going well, but the real test is when the trials come. God blessed us for our faithfulness in worship and prayer, yes! But more so, because we also chose to put our trust in Him with our hearts <u>and</u> <u>our</u> <u>tithe</u>; it gave Him an opportunity to prove His faithfulness to us! I believe that it is in that kind of circumstances that God finds great pleasure!

I cannot over emphasize; how essential it is to maintain an acute awareness that the real test of being willing to stand on Faith is when the going gets tough!

Remember what the Lord said,

> *Romans 8:24-25 (NIV)*
> *24 For in this hope we were saved. But hope that is seen is no hope at all. Who hopes for*

what they already have? 25 But if we hope
for what we do not yet have, we wait for it
patiently.

Here is a prime example of Faith Standing:
 When Job was in the thick of Satan's attack on his life, he was tempted even by "friends" to curse God and doubt His faithfulness. But Job knew in whom he believed, and he was completely and totally persuaded in his faith. He was sold out to the fact that God *was* able to keep him! He was committed to trust in God's faithfulness. In other words, Job knew that no matter what the circumstances, and whether God restored him now during his earthly life or ended His life on this earth and took him to heaven, God was his deliverer either way! Did he get angry with God? Yes! But did he quit trusting and standing on Faith before God? NO!

It's a choice! Faith is a choice; not a magic potion that we beg God for. Not something that He feeds to us in small doses every few hours, or every few days or years!

Faith is the "substance" –
Merriam-Webster refers to "Substance" as:

- A natural "Essence"

- A fundamental or Characteristic part or quality

- Ultimate reality that underlies all outward manifestations and change…

120

The Essence of what you stand for and what you act on! Simply because you have made that choice to believe and trust in it!

When we truly believe in something, we not only strive to focus our life on that belief standard; but we want our friends to find the beauty in it also. "The substance of things hoped for…" What do you hope for? "The evidence of things not seen…"
The actions that you take, based on your belief, is what makes the difference in your life and Faith! You say you need more Faith? What are you doing with the measure you already have?

God is faithful, and as you grow to know Him better you will come into a full realization of that fact! Your ability to trust Him will become more like second nature! The fact is, after all is said and done, shouldn't that be our desire?

As He puts a song in my heart, today I sing:

My Hope is built on nothing less,

than Jesus' blood and righteousness,

I dare not trust the sweetest frame

But wholly lean on Jesus name!

On Christ the Solid Rock I Stand!...

I have experienced the results of

Faith... Standing....

and you know something?...

...I like it!

Jeremiah 17:8
  For he shall be as a tree planted
by the waters, and that spreadeth
  out her roots by the river, and
 shall not see when heat cometh,
  but her leaf shall be green; and
 shall not be careful in the year of
 drought, neither shall cease from
        yielding fruit.

There is not darkness enough in all the world
to put out the light of one little candle. – Epitaph

Psalm 85:10-11

Unfailing love and truth have met together. Righteousness and peace have kissed! Truth springs up from the earth, and righteousness smiles down from heaven.

I John 5:20

And we know that the son of God has come, and he has given us understanding so that we can know the true god. And now we live in fellowship with his son, Jesus Christ. He is the only true God, and he is eternal life.

Finale - But Not the Last Stand...

Last notes and thoughts:

Along this journey I experienced some of the most trying challenges in my life. Temptations to just quit were strong and frequent. The struggles were so hard at times that I considered the thought that, "perhaps if I quit now, the troubles will go away, and I can live in peace!"

You see, I thought the writing of this book was the biggest part of the journey. However, I realize in hindsight that it was only the beginning!

As I came to the completion of the writing part and began to seriously contemplate publishing, so many emotional, mental and even physical struggles hit me that I began to question the validity of my own Faith and ability to stand!

But, deep in my spirit I knew the real truth! I knew that God had met my needs so many times and had indeed spoken to my heart. I knew He was with me all the way, so; I kept moving along, trusting God to bring me through it and I refused to give up!

One day recently, as I gave a great big sigh of exasperation due to the pain I had been suffering; The bible story of Job began to fill my thoughts. Of course, I instantly said, oh Lord What I'm going through has been hard, but my suffering does not begin to compare with Job!

But my mind was still brought to Job!

Job was a righteous man yet suffered more than any of us dare to imagine! He believed and trusted God, no matter what! Despite the discouragements, losses, anger and pain! When he lost it all, he still continued to trust God and take a stand of faith that God would bring him through it all and restore to him what was taken! God not only brought him through it, but He restored what was taken from Job, multiplied!

How much do we endure before our faith and trust in God falters? How long will you trust God before you take hold and try to control it all over again? How willing are you to take that strong stand, just like the old oak tree?

Since the completion of writing Faith Standing, I was blessed to discover additional learning tools lying within the life of the oak tree! Our Heavenly Father has provided so many signs and wonders of His Glory throughout the earth! Why do I ever doubt Him?!

You will go out in joy and be led forth in peace; the mountains and hills will burst into song before you, and all the trees of the field will clap their hands.

Isaiah 55:12

The Mighty Oak
(True Story)
By Lu Scrogan

It's Called The Mighty Oak Tree,
for it grows so big and strong
Its branches stretch and seem to dance
and wave to each wind's song
As the storm blows loud trumpets,
the Oak resists not it's wind,
but allows it to pass through clearly,
not causing the Oak to bend
The leaves resist being ripped by winds,
that would tear them right away
They curl like a cylinder shape
allowing winds to pass as they sway
When an enemy comes charging in,
aiming his arrow at you
Step aside and wave him past;
you've better things to do!
Don't focus on him or acknowledge his plight
He just wants to pull you down into a fight
Don't give him attention, not even time of day!
Be gone in the name of Jesus! Is all you need say!
When he whispers threats and discouragements,
just turn and walk away
Why wrestle with the devil,
just take that time to pray!
And what's more...

...To listen to that liar, to give an ear to him
Puts the battle in your hands and
leaves you out on a limb
When the great storm Katrina
tried to uproot the oaks
They indeed rooted in deeper,
but ...listen and hear dear folks...
Each oak is not an island, it does not stand as one
For Oaks weave their roots together and
that's how they've won!
For when all that had been standing there
was leveled to the ground;
The Mighty Oaks, were left there
standing all around!
So, as the winds blow more fiercely, and
you feel you're out on the rim
Remember to weave in with others
that also believe in Him!
For Standing alone is harder,
standing together is best
Either way, God is good so put
Faith Standing to the test!
Yes, the Mighty Oak Stands Strong!

As the battle rages on,
Just remember that the battle is the Lord's,
not yours!

By Lu Scrogan

Weave in and Stand!

By Lu Scrogan

The battle is hard... The struggle is real...

To give up is often the way that I feel.

To reach up seems daunting...

To reach out too bleak...

My heart is too heavy,

My arms are too weak

But look!...

There is a root system, into which you can weave

Where others can stand with you and believe

No man is an Island...

So, don't try to be!

Weave deep into the blessings

just like the oak tree...

and just stand!